THE IMAGE OF LEADERSHIP IN SERVICE & DUTY

Revised and Expanded Edition
10th Anniversary

THE IMAGE OF LEADERSHIP IN SERVICE & DUTY

How Leaders in Government & Public Service Package Themselves to Stand Out for All the Right Reasons

by
Sylvie di Giusto

ISBN: 979-8-9901927-8-2

To the defenders of progress, justice, and security
who serve with honor, lead with courage,
and uphold the values that unite and protect us all.

Contents

About This Special Edition

Ten years ago I released my first book, *The Image of Leadership*, not fully grasping the impact it would have on my own career trajectory. At that time, I remember feeling a mix of excitement and nervousness. After all, releasing a book into the world is no small feat. Just a few weeks before I hit that "Publish" button, and while I was still overthinking every single word, Mark Sanborn, a titan of leadership thought, bestselling author, and Hall of Fame speaker himself, gave me a piece of advice that has stayed with me: "Nobody cares about your first book, but everybody cares that you have a first book." In the speaking world, a book is an entry point, a business card, a conversation starter, a testament to your thoughts and expertise. So I published it.

That first book did, indeed, open doors, spark conversations, and lead to speaking engagements, fulfilling its role perfectly—and much more. But Mark wasn't finished. He turned around and, while walking off, threw a greater challenge my way: "But you really must write a good second book, Sylvie." So consider this updated and expanded edition of *The Image of Leadership* my "second good book," the refined version of my initial offering.

Much has changed in ten years. The digital landscape has evolved rapidly with the rise of mobile technology, social media, and artificial intelligence transforming the ways we work and connect. Casual work attire has become more accepted, reflecting a shift toward prioritizing comfort and individuality in the workplace. Diversity and inclusion have taken center stage with a growing recognition of the importance of creating equitable work environments.

The global marketplace has become increasingly interconnected, requiring leaders to navigate cultural differences and build international relationships regularly. And we can't forget the profound impact of the pandemic that accelerated the adoption of remote work and virtual collaboration. For a while it was clear *The Image of Leadership* needed more than just a touch-up; it needed a full makeover to reflect these seismic shifts and provide guidance for leaders navigating this new landscape. It needed a comprehensive renewal to stay relevant in a world that has shifted so fundamentally.

And so I embarked on a journey of complete revision rather than mere superficial changes. This journey wasn't just about updating; it was about reimagining and realigning the book with the times we live in.

Although I have maintained the book's original structure and focus, over the past ten years I also have had the privilege of speaking to a variety of leaders in service and duty sectors. From military commanders to first responders, from government officials to law enforcement officers, those exchanges were two-way streets. For every insight I've offered from the stage, I've received an equal measure of wisdom from my audiences. The specific challenges they've shared, the questions they've asked, and the stories they've told have deepened my understanding and approach to leadership.

I'm immensely thankful for this reciprocal learning. It's this exchange that has breathed new life into *The Image of Leadership,* transforming it into an edition that reflects not just my voice but also the collective wisdom of the many dedicated professionals in service and duty roles I've engaged with.

This reciprocal learning has been one of the greatest gifts of my career; and among the many distinguished leaders I have had the privilege of meeting, Chief Oliver Pu-Folkes stands out as an extraordinary force in law enforcement and public service. Years ago, I was not just taken by surprise but truly honored when Chief Pu-Folkes approached me and shared that he had been following my work.

He had even read the original version of *The Image of Leadership*, incorporated its principles into his leadership development efforts, and ensured his team members had access to its lessons. When he later invited me to NYPD headquarters, the very heart of one of the world's most renowned law- enforcement agencies, I was given a rare, behind-the-scenes glimpse into how the leaders of this city safeguard its people, institutions, and future.

Since then, Chief Pu-Folkes' journey has taken him from shaping the next generation of NYPD officers to serving in a pivotal role as chief investigator for the New York State Attorney General's Office, where he continues to uphold the highest standards of integrity, accountability, and leadership. He generously made it possible for me to have the privilege of sharing my insights with the investigators of this agency—and once again, it was a testament to the power of reciprocal learning and the continuous exchange of knowledge that defines my work. While I was there in the role of a speaker, the insights shared with me by Chief Pu-Folkes, his team, and the investigators had a lasting impact on me, shaping my understanding in profound ways. Through their experiences, I gained a deeper knowledge of unconscious bias in investigative work, the complexities of decision-making in high-stakes public service roles, the ethical considerations that guide their work, and the immense responsibility they carry in safeguarding justice and public trust.

So having Chief Pu-Folkes write the foreword for this edition is an immense honor. His name is synonymous with leadership, his reputation built on decades of dedicated service, and his legacy marked by the countless lives he has influenced. He is not only a guardian of justice but also a mentor, a strategist, and a standard-bearer for ethical leadership in public service. His insights set the perfect stage for this book, and I am profoundly grateful for his contributions—both to this work and to the countless professionals who look up to him as an example of what true leadership should be, including myself.

So here's to those leaders who embody resilience and dedication every day. This resource is for you. Whether you're a military officer, a law enforcement commander, an emergency services coordinator, or a government executive, let this book be your guide to navigating the high stakes and unique challenges of your professional journey.

But it's more than that. This book is also a thank-you for your dedication across all sectors of public service as well as a tool to aid your journey forward, whether you're engaging with team members or the public face-to-face, over the phone, or online. It's a recognition of the leaders who are shaping the future of communities and operations, one decision at a time. Consider this book the "second" that Mark Sanborn urged me to perfect, a version refined by experience and honed by the passage of time, a handbook for the present, a road map for the future, and a testament to the enduring power of a leader's professional identity that transcends the diverse landscapes of service and duty.

Mine is a deeply personal thank-you, one that holds a special place in my heart. You see, as I celebrated the tenth anniversary of the original *Image of Leadership,* I decided to commemorate this milestone with ten special editions, each tailored to the leaders I've had the honor of engaging over the years. From real estate to hospitality, from healthcare to the technology sector, I've tried to capture the essence of leadership across the sectors that have shaped my professional journey. But one thing was always clear: the final edition would be dedicated to you, an extraordinary group of leaders who helped me fulfill a lifelong dream.

Let me explain. I have a brother who is ten years older than I, and he once told me that, when I was five, someone asked me the classic question, "What do you want to be when you grow up?" While other children eagerly answered "I want to be a teacher," or "I want to be a doctor," without missing a beat, my answer was both surprising and clear: "I want to be an American."

Growing up in Europe with a multicultural background, I always cherished the richness and diversity of my upbringing, but I never quite felt at home.

For reasons I couldn't fully explain, a love for the United States was imprinted on me from as far back as I—or my brother—could remember. That dream of being an American stayed with me for decades, unwavering and persistent, despite countless setbacks and failed attempts that left it feeling out of reach.

But then one day, in the most unexpected turn of events, my dream came true. With a newborn in my arms, I boarded a plane and moved to the land of limitless opportunity. The United States, a country I had admired for so long, finally became my home. I went through the journey of visas, green cards and, eventually—and proudly—citizenship—each step a deeply personal commitment to the country I had always dreamed of calling my own. And now I am one of those dreamers whose dream never could have been realized without the work you do. Your leadership, your service, your dedication to protecting and upholding the ideals of this nation are the foundation that made it possible for me to build a life here, a life that now feels whole, a life that finally feels like home.

My gratitude for you, your work, and this country is immeasurable. So despite all the advice and consultations from editors, agencies, and publishers I knew, without a doubt, that the last and final special edition of *The Image of Leadership* would be for you.

May this updated edition serve you as a beacon through the ever-changing landscape of service and duty leadership, inspiring you to continue making impactful decisions with confidence, purpose, and authority. And may it remind you that each of your choices can change your life, the lives of your team members, or the life of someone in the public—someone like me.

Foreword by Oliver Pu-Folkes

The final special edition of Sylvie's original book, *The Image of Leadership*, is a honed work that contextualizes leadership from the framework of "Service & Duty." These are powerful ideals that separate those who enter government work from those who pursue private sector business—where the bottom line is measured by what one can offer in service to others. These people are motivated by honor and duty rather than being motivated and measuring success by what one can gain by maximization of a company's profits.

Government has long been saddled with the reputation that those who seek, enter, or remain within this noble profession, even with good intentions, will find it an environment that is ill-suited to innovation and creativity. In addition, most come to find that it is infused with bureaucracy and status quo defenders and where "fitting in" is preferred to "standing out." However, the best way to change this image is to be the change you wish to see—an empowering perspective that in the years ahead I would come to find in the chapters of *The Image of Leadership*. Each chapter constituted an encyclopedia of well researched and developed ideas that most precisely captured and crystalized my longstanding viewpoint that government actors—from the front lines to top executives— can be "the CEO of their own image" by influencing and inspiring the public through better managing their individual appearance, behavior, communication, digital presence, and environment.

Too often government, especially in a paramilitary organization such as my first agency, the New York City Police Department (NYPD), is hierarchal, favors strict adherence to chain-of-command, and expects both conformity and uniformity within the organization from the bottom up. The unintentional consequence of this model often prevents front- line uniformed and nonuniformed personnel from taking ownership of their professional identity. It also prevents them from understanding that leading—which is persuading or influencing others regardless of whether others are positionally placed above, below, or laterally in terms of power dynamics—does not require an organization's conferral of a promotion in rank or title.

The concept of leadership captures the explosive idea that at any level or position within government, rather than wait and hope for a promotion that can only be gained by a combination of competitive examination placement and the discretion of higher ranking decision-makers, one can have individual agency to essentially promote oneself through full adoption of the ideas contained in *The Image of Leadership*.

My personal journey in public service started as an NYPD police officer in the late 1980s. I entered the force as a proud lifelong New Yorker who witnessed the harm of the crack-cocaine epidemic that touched many communities, families, and individuals. I moved up the ranks within the police department and later went on to serve in several senior executive government-appointed positions at the city and state levels, serving at the pleasure of elected officials.

I have no doubt that the positions of service and duty that I enjoyed were offered because wearing the image of leadership fits better than any uniform I ever donned. From this posture, there is opportunity for a career that is punctuated by remarkability—measured by our capacity to impact and improve the lives of others. We can achieve this when we live and breathe our professional identities as an intact image that best reflects an agency's mission and values.

As the United States undergoes a change of leadership at the helm of the seat of power, part of the perpetual swing between red and blue, we must all come together to repair the divide of the American people by political affiliation to instead reemphasize our shared values of democracy and American grit.

For this reason, government leaders of all ranks, titles, and positions at the federal, state, and local levels must continue to better meet the needs of the public, build the trust of the communities served, and exemplify the best of American democratic ideology in a nonpartisan way. As *The Image of Leadership in Service & Duty* emphasizes, we can achieve the goals and objectives of good government by recognizing that we are not passive observers of governance but empowered actors able to lead our nation by accepting individual responsibility for conducting the work of the people with a consistent image of leadership. I strongly recommend to my colleagues, especially in the field of public safety and law enforcement, that this special edition should be required reading for all committed government agents.

Oliver Pu-Folkes
Chief Investigator, New York State Attorney General

Introduction

Welcome to The Image of Leadership. The title reflects the reality that every leader can and should acknowledge—that true leadership manifests itself in ways that are both seen and unseen, and they're equally important. Even though leaders have their own individual styles and personalities, it cannot be doubted that the most effective leaders, the ones who succeed over long periods, are seen and accepted because their interior skills and exterior images are in perfect alignment. In other words, what you see is what you get. Leaders must be consistent and dependable, and their professional identity—which I'll introduce to you later in the book—must be strong and durable.

Whether you're preparing to take on your first leadership role, have just been promoted to a commanding position, or have spent years leading teams in the field, at the helm of an agency, or on the frontlines of public service, you may wonder, "Is this book for me?"

My answer is yes; this book is definitely for you. It's crafted not only for the aspiring leader but also for the seasoned senior leader. Regardless of the landscape—whether you stand as a solitary figure in a command center, agency office, or operational field or as part of a growing network of leaders—this book is a beacon for your journey that illuminates the ways you can solidify your professional identity and shape your leadership narrative.

It's designed to instill a culture of excellence and leadership at every level because, whether you're just starting your leadership journey with aspirations for a pivotal role in public safety, government operations, or defense strategy, or you're a seasoned professional making pivotal decisions about teams, operations, or

community outcomes, the way you present yourself should consistently reflect the leader you aspire to be.

The dynamics might differ—navigating the complexities of agency hierarchies, responding to mission-critical tasks, or managing interagency collaborations—yet the core principle remains the same: whether you're at the threshold of your career or you're a seasoned professional, the way you present yourself should consistently reflect the leader you aspire to be.

The life-or-death decisions during deployments, the pivotal discussions within leadership meetings about policies, the charged atmosphere of major strategic decisions, or the choices made on the ground in high-pressure environments—all these scenarios demand leaders who possess not only the expertise but also the professional identity and gravitas to instill confidence and inspire change.

This book will take you step-by-step through the development of this professional identity. The focus will be on all the things people perceive about you with an emphasis on your "look of leadership," your image, what others see and experience as you lead a briefing with your teams or articulate your vision for your agency to the public. This focus is based on the proven concept that you cannot simply tell others you're a leader and expect them to treat you as one. You must show others your leadership every day in a way that encourages them to instantly accept you as someone they will trust.

Although this book focuses on the way you represent yourself internally to your teams or to your own senior leaders, I want to remind you that maintaining all these principles is also vital when interacting with external stakeholders. As a leader you're always "on stage," not just in team briefings or command meetings. Every interaction matters, whether it's a presentation to potential collaborators, an event at a policy summit, a speaking engagement at an interagency conference, a meeting with public officials, or your engagement within your local community. Your professional identity is constantly being shaped and reinforced by how you present yourself in each of those moments.

Remember, everyone is watching you all the time, and your interactions in every situation contribute to the overall perception of your leadership. Only by being mindful of this fact can you ensure your professional identity is cohesive, consistent, and impactful, no matter the context.

We'll begin with the seven-second rule. This is that critical moment when others first encounter you. They may have some prior knowledge of you, but this is the first time they actually lay eyes on you. I'll show you how others make up their minds quickly about your leadership potential and either open the door for you or slam it shut. The good thing is that this process is entirely under your control. Within those first micro-moments you can choose to present yourself as a leader or not.

Next, we'll dive into the powerful undercurrents of the human mind and explore how, even after those initial micro-moments, other people's perceptions and judgments about you can be influenced in profound ways by using tools you already have. You can control the components of your professional identity—the ABCDEs of your professional presence: appearance, behavior, communication, digital footprint, and environment.

Although all the components of the ABCDEs are crucial and only work effectively when they intersect and interplay, we'll focus on how you're perceived visually. But please note that this isn't a fashion guide. I'm not going to detail specific items of clothing or accessories you need to buy and wear. Instead, I want to provide a deep understanding of the concepts you need to put into practice in your own way. I want to give you the power to create your own professional identity, one that's true to your personality, that works for the duration of your career, that stands as a testament to the sector you're a part of and, by extension, the communities you serve.

We'll also delve deeper into the area of your digital leadership. In an age when your digital presence is as crucial as your in-person interactions, we'll explore how to cultivate a compelling digital footprint that reinforces your leadership identity in the sector and beyond. From leveraging social media platforms to crafting a

powerful online narrative, you'll learn strategies to control and extend your influence and establish yourself as a thought leader in the digital sphere.

Although this book is focused on helping you refine your professional identity, you'll also develop a deeper understanding of how and why some of your teams may struggle to apply the elements of their ABCDEs effectively. As you read through these pages, you'll find yourself identifying areas where you and your teams can grow together. For addressing sensitive issues with teams, I'll equip you with the tools and techniques to approach those difficult conversations with confidence and grace. You'll learn how to communicate with empathy, assert your authority when necessary, and foster a culture of open and constructive dialogue within your teams because, as a leader, your success is intrinsically tied to your ability to inspire and guide others. Hence, we'll explore the art of leading by example, showcasing how your decisions set the tone for your entire agency. Only by embodying the qualities you seek to instill in others will you create a ripple effect of positive change.

In crafting this book it was important to recognize that leaders' experiences and identities are vast and diverse. That's why this book is committed to embracing every leader, regardless of their background or of the unique challenges they face in their particular sector.

Here, every leader is welcome and valued. Leaders come in all genders, shapes, sizes, ages, styles, and levels—including yours. I hope this book will help you develop your professional identity on your journey of becoming the leader you deserve to be. It's all a matter of letting others see that your inner star is ready to shine.

It's also important to mention that inclusive language was a priority in crafting this book. On one hand I wanted to ensure that every leader, regardless of their role, rank, or background feels seen and valued in these pages.

But on the other hand, I also recognized the importance of simplicity and readability. Your sector encompasses a wide variety of terms and structures, from teams to units, from departments to

divisions, from agencies to commands, so I've chosen to simplify wherever possible. For instance, I use the term "teams" to represent everyone working under your leadership, whether they are unit members, personnel, or staff. Similarly, I use "agencies" as a universal term for the diverse entities you may lead, whether they are government agencies, departments, or other institutions within your sector.

This intentional simplification helps keep the book accessible and relatable while respecting the nuances of your roles. Thank you for understanding this approach, and I hope you find the content as practical and impactful as it is inclusive.

So let's get started on this exciting journey to achieving your full leadership potential.

Love,
Sylvie

Chapter 1
Seven Seconds

Seven Seconds:
Just a Glimpse,
but the Vision Lasts.

1 2 3 4 5 6 7

Chapter 1: Seven Seconds

Appearance matters. Every hour of every day, we evaluate our environment based on what we see and hear. We avoid situations and individuals that seem threatening. We gravitate toward situations and individuals that appear welcoming. When we meet someone we use sensory information to quickly determine whether we're going to get along with them or if we need to keep our distance. We turn on the television and say, "This show looks good. I think I'll watch it." At the store, we inspect the food we want to buy. When a dog approaches us on the street, before we extend our hand, we examine its body language. Is the tail wagging, or is the dog tense? Similarly, we enter an agency office or operational base and instantly assess the atmosphere, evaluating the demeanor of the team members we encounter. We attend a community forum and quickly gauge the organization of the event by observing the efficiency of its registration process. We meet an official for the first time and form an impression within moments based on their posture, handshake, and tone of voice. Whether it's a briefing room, a deployment site, or an interagency conference, these first impressions are inevitable and impactful.

We all do it—me and you—whether we want to, whether we're aware of it, or even if we think we're above it. And just as we judge others, we're judged by the people who meet us or see us. Do we appear trustworthy and confident? Or do we appear uncertain or detached? Are we seen as decisive and capable of leading a team through mission-critical situations?

Do we project an image of approachability that encourages open communication and collaboration? Are we viewed as inspirational leaders who motivate and uplift in the high-stakes world of service and duty? Or are we seen as authoritarian figures who instill fear rather than respect?

These initial perceptions influence the decisions people make about us. Should they trust us to lead a task force, assign us to command a high-stakes operation, follow our lead in implementing new protocols, or collaborate with us on critical interagency initiatives?

Research supports this idea of initial perceptions. Some studies suggest it takes mere milliseconds to form those perceptions while others say it takes three, seven, or eleven seconds to delineate the characteristics people use to judge us.

In my professional work I've focused on the study suggesting that judgment takes place within seven seconds. Those seven seconds, and the research I rely on in my work, are based on a study conducted by Dr. Michael Solomon, a psychologist at NYU. His work suggests our initial imprint is not based on a single element; instead, it is a composite of at least eleven elements that others subconsciously use to judge us within those first moments when we meet. Those elements are as follows:

- Socioeconomic level
- Education level
- Competence and honesty, believability, and perceived credibility
- Sex role identification
- Level of sophistication
- Trustworthiness
- Level of success
- Ethnicity
- Religious background
- Political background
- Social/sexual/professional desirability

Yet, it's imperative to approach this list with a discerning mind. On one enlightening occasion I had the honor of conversing with Dr. Solomon, and he shared a significant point with me: Like many scientific findings, the interpretations of his study have been bent to fit various narratives across the internet and by other self-proclaimed "experts." It's one of those pervasive myths that human judgment rigidly conforms to the eleven-elements and seven-seconds rules. Yet, the study never confirmed that assumption and has consistently been taken out of context. Dr. Solomon even shared that the study, as it's usually portrayed on the internet, never actually took place. This is a powerful reminder for all of us to avoid taking information from the internet at face value and to always verify the original sources.

So while I won't delve into the specifics of the study or its misrepresentations found online, it's important to understand the broader implications. Regardless of which study you examine, they all have one thing in common: This process of judgment occurs automatically in our brains, whether we're aware of it, whether we find it fair, or whether, under our uniforms or titles, we carry the soul of Mother Teresa.

Think about it this way: When a team member meets you for the first time, they're not instantly evaluating your leadership skills or your strategic plans for mission success or operational improvements. They're evaluating you as a person. They're asking themselves, *Is this someone I can trust? Is this someone who understands my needs? Is this someone who's professional, knowledgeable, and reliable?* Before a team member makes the decision to follow you as a leader, they first need to "buy into you."

Similarly, when a stakeholder or member of the public meets you for the first time, they are not immediately assessing the protocols you've designed or the operational efficiencies you've implemented. They're observing you and wondering, *Is this someone who will address my concerns? Is this someone who is attentive and trustworthy? Is this someone who will ensure my needs are taken seriously and my concerns addressed with professionalism?*

Before they feel assured in your leadership, they need to feel confident in your attentiveness and commitment to their well-being. Your look of leadership provides the first clues to answering their questions. Of course, appearance alone isn't enough. You also need to have the substance to back it up. This means demonstrating your expertise, reliability, and value through various actions over time: your deep understanding of your agency's mission and responsibilities, your ability to ask insightful questions and provide tailored solutions to address challenges, your prompt and effective follow-up on team or public concerns, and your commitment to delivering impactful results. But in those crucial first moments your appearance sets the stage for the relationship. It's the foundation trust is built on.

Anyone who aspires to a position of leadership in any capacity in the service and duty sector needs to understand the power of their visual presence. And the good news is that this is something you can control. You can make it what you want.

Let's start with a story about two professionals, Evan and Matt, both aiming for a key leadership position within a federal law enforcement agency. They're competing for the position of regional operations director, a critical role overseeing multiagency collaboration and managing high-stakes field operations.

First, let's meet Evan. Brimming with anticipation, he waits in the reception area of the agency's regional headquarters. Christine, the Deputy Director of Federal Operations, arrives to greet him. As one of the highest-ranking officials within the agency, Christine oversees strategic initiatives across multiple regions and plays a pivotal role in shaping national policy implementation. With a confident smile that's both formal and businesslike, she shakes Evan's hand firmly before leading him toward her office.

As they walk through the corridors, they pass clusters of special agents coordinating field operations and intelligence analysts reviewing mission-critical data. An uneasy silence grows between Evan and Christine. Upon arriving at her expansive office, Christine gestures for Evan to take a seat. She moves to her side of the desk and, with a brief smile, scans Evan's résumé.

Her questions are precise, delving into Evan's successes in leading task forces and exploring the distinctive skills he would bring to this high-level role.

During the interview Evan begins to feel out of sync. While his credentials are solid and landed him the interview, he senses Christine is searching for something more. He speculates that her composed demeanor reflects a high level of detachment, a necessary trait for someone at her rank. Evan starts doubting whether he's making a meaningful connection with her.

After twenty minutes, Christine closes Evan's file and looks up. "Do you have any questions for me?" Evan hesitates, thrown off by her reserved demeanor. Although he has a multitude of questions about the agency's plans for enhancing interagency collaboration and modernizing operational strategies, he says he has no questions at the moment and, instead, inquires about the next steps.

"As I'm sure you'll understand," Christine says, "we have a significant number of candidates for this role. This initial interview is just the start of the process. We'll be in touch by next week." Christine thanks him politely and shows him to the door. As Evan exits, he senses that his chances for a callback are slim.

Now let's meet Matt. On paper, his qualifications are nearly identical to Evan's. Like Evan, Matt is vying for the role of regional operations director, a position that would mark a major step forward in his career as well. Matt's experience begins the same way as Evan's. Christine greets him in the reception area with the same firm handshake and professional demeanor. But during the brief walk through the corridors, Matt engages Christine in light conversation. "Deputy Director, it's a privilege to meet you," he says. "I've followed some of your work in developing the National Task Force on Cybersecurity Collaboration. The progress your team made was impressive."

Christine glances at him, her interest piqued. "That initiative was a collective effort. I'm glad to hear it resonated with you. Did you have an interest in cybersecurity initiatives during your current role?"

When they arrive at Christine's office, Matt takes his seat with an air of confidence, and Christine reviews his résumé. Her questions are just as precise as they were with Evan. When she asks about his approach to enhancing operational efficiency, Matt references specific examples of his leadership in streamlining interagency communications during emergency response scenarios.

Christine leans forward, intrigued by Matt's insight. When he mentions his ideas for incorporating emerging technologies to improve decision-making in the field, Christine invites a senior advisor on technology integration to join their conversation. Matt uses the opportunity to display his understanding of the complexities involved in deploying new tools while maintaining operational readiness.

After an hour, Christine glances at her schedule with slight regret. "Matt, I'd like to continue this conversation. Are you available for a follow-up meeting next week?" Matt eagerly says yes and expresses his appreciation for the engaging discussion. As he leaves, Matt feels a surge of confidence. He has not only connected with Christine but also has left a positive impression on another key leader within the agency.

The next day Christine convenes a leadership meeting to discuss the candidates for the regional operations director role. When Evan's name comes up, Christine's assessment is decisive. "He's qualified, but I didn't see the level of engagement or strategic thinking we need for this position," she says. Then it's Matt's turn. "Impressive," Christine remarks. "He demonstrated a strong command of our priorities and articulated innovative ideas that align with our vision. He would be an excellent fit."

Evan and Matt, two capable leaders with equivalent qualifications. Yet, in the eyes of Christine, one seemed mismatched, the other distinguished.

If you were to ask Christine what made the difference, she might not directly say it was, for instance, the way they presented themselves that set one apart from the other—next to, of course, many other factors.

But in the service and duty sector where someone's professional identity can reflect an individual's meticulousness and diligence in leading teams through high-pressure situations, the way they presented themselves might have played a crucial role. Even if he was dressed appropriately, it could have been Evan's unadorned suit (lacking a hint of individuality) or his conservative accessories (missing a spark of confidence) that failed to imprint upon Christine the image of a dynamic, compelling leader beneath an otherwise unremarkable exterior. She may not acknowledge that her opinion of Evan was formed from the moment she saw him in the reception area, dressed understated, leisurely seated, his posture a little too relaxed, his gaze idly locked on his smartphone, scarcely aware of the activity around him. His apparent lack of engagement with his surroundings might have inadvertently suggested an absence of readiness or drive that is prized in the demanding world of service and duty leadership.

The interview? It might have been just an obligation, a formality. Evan may never have had a chance. As soon as she could, Christine cut the interview short and showed him the door.

In both recruitment and senior leadership circles, the instant perception of a candidate is often an unspoken consideration. Although it may be regarded as trivial and go unacknowledged as part of the formal evaluation process, that instant perception often does play a part in decision-making.

Furthermore, legal and ethical standards prevent citing an instant perception as a reason for employment decisions. Christine won't explicitly say, "We can't bring you into our leadership team because your external presentation doesn't align with our expectations." Such a statement would cross professional boundaries and could lead to significant repercussions.

Likewise, she cannot acknowledge that she may have formed opinions about the candidates before they even met, influenced by the credentials and images presented in their online personas. Nonetheless, the reality is that, in any environment, the impression made by a person's visual presence can subtly influence the final employment decision.

The principles illustrated in this story go well beyond just the job interview. They're also highly relevant in interactions with external stakeholders, team members, and colleagues across a variety of service and duty leadership scenarios.

When interacting with external stakeholders, whether it's resolving a concern in a community meeting, providing a briefing to interagency collaborators, or responding to public inquiries, the impression you make influences their trust in your leadership and your agency's mission.

The impression you make applies to presentations in team briefings, interagency discussions, and any team-facing activities you engage in. Even in casual conversations or informal meetings with your field officers, technical teams, or administrative team, the impression you make shapes their overall view of your capabilities.

While your skills, knowledge, and results are paramount, the subtle yet powerful cues of your presence frequently influence your team's or stakeholders' subconscious impressions of your expertise, diligence, and potential value. It shapes their openness to your influence, guidance, and leadership.

A well-curated look of leadership sends a message of competence and dependability, establishing trust from the moment you step into a room. It's not just about looking good; it's about demonstrating respect for your role, your agency, and the people you lead. Each detail of your presentation speaks volumes and can be as pivotal to team morale or stakeholder confidence as the strategic insights you provide or the decisions you make.

The adage says, "You can't judge a book by its cover." Yet the hard reality is, every day, in countless interactions, leaders are judged by their "covers." It may not be fair, but doing so is an intrinsic human instinct. Although we encourage looking beyond the surface, there often isn't enough time for others to form opinions based on deep observation.

Remember, the exact amount of time—three seconds or seven—doesn't matter. Such a brief window is not enough for people to thoroughly assess your capabilities or leadership qualities.

That's why their brain defaults to the path of least resistance, the most straightforward route for gathering information—their eyes. Humans are, after all, visual creatures.

Just imagine walking into your first team meeting. Until you get settled, you don't have much time to persuade with facts and figures about strategy or mission outcomes. The team's first impression of you is dictated primarily by how you carry yourself and your overall presence. Or think about joining a virtual meeting with your team or interagency collaborators. Before you even begin speaking about operational priorities or updates, they have already subconsciously evaluated your appearance, body language, facial expressions, or the setup behind you. Now consider interacting with a stakeholder during a community engagement event. Before you can highlight your agency's efforts or initiatives, the stakeholder has already formed an impression based on your professional demeanor before they even experience the full scope of your leadership.

Those visuals shape perceptions before you can deliver your strategic insights or solutions. Even when sending emails or posting messages in digital channels, any visual elements associated with your outreach contribute to whether a stakeholder or team member sees you as someone credible and worth engaging further. Your email signature, the fonts you use, any emojis you add, your profile picture—each sets the tone for your leadership identity.

Research led by Doug Vogel at the University of Arizona illuminated the speed at which our brains process images—60,000 times faster than text—and asserted that 90 percent of information is transmitted visually. Further emphasizing the predominance of visual information, Dr. Mary Potter from MIT led a study that found the human brain can process images seen for as little as thirteen milliseconds. This rapid processing suggests our brains are constantly and efficiently working to understand the visual world around us. These astounding facts highlight the immediate impact of visual cues on our perception, making your appearance a powerful communication tool.

Think about it: Before you've even spoken a word in a meeting, your visual presence has already conveyed a wealth of information. It's not just your clothing your audience subconsciously studies, it's your body language, facial expressions, eye contact, gestures, the way you enter the room, carry yourself, or the energy you project—all are visual cues that communicate volumes.

Imagine a concerned community member standing in a public forum. As you walk toward the person, you are being assessed on your level of attentiveness and willingness to help. Your posture, facial expression, and speed at which you move all contribute to the initial impression of whether you will address their concerns effectively or not.

Or perhaps you've experienced firsthand how visually driven we are. Have you ever spoken to someone on the phone and, based solely on their voice, formed a mental image of what they might look like and then, upon meeting them in person, been surprised when they didn't match your vision?

At the interview Evan might have believed, based on his experience, that his monochromatic look was neutral enough to be acceptable. But the moment Christine first scrutinized him, her internal judgment was clear. She might have thought, consciously or subconsciously, *This candidate doesn't grasp the dynamic essence of this role's responsibilities, and I don't have time to teach him.* Of course, it's possible that in a different agency or for another leadership position Evan's look or conduct would not have been a pivotal factor. But for Christine's standards and the particular role she sought in regional operations leadership, Evan was not the right fit.

And your team members might think something similar: *This leader doesn't understand or align with our mission and values. If they can't represent themselves properly, how can I trust them to guide us in achieving our objectives?* They may, consciously or subconsciously, wonder if your lackluster professional identity is indicative of the kind of mediocre leadership they could expect when collaborating on critical operations or implementing initiatives.

Whether interacting with team members, senior leaders, or the public, the split-second visual analysis of "Does this person embody the qualities we're seeking in a leader?" can overrule the other positive attributes you bring to the table. Others may dismiss you before fully appreciating the value you could provide simply because the initial visual cues didn't instill the right level of confidence in you.

Just as we judge products based on their packaging, wines on their labels, or movies on their trailers, team members and the public judge leaders through the lens of their own requirements and environments. The subtle cues of a leader's visual presence are filtered through their perceptions of what an ideal leader should look and act like. A mismatch can lead to disqualification before even getting to deal with your core competencies.

As for Matt, the moment Christine saw him—even before they shook hands—she knew he was a contender. His tailored suit, his confident posture, his poised demeanor, and his purposeful energy—all were indicative of a candidate who viewed himself as a leader ready to take on strategic challenges. And not just any leader, but one who could resonate with the dynamic and high-stakes demands of the role.

It might have been his ability to blend formality with approachability or the way he effortlessly combined professional demeanor with a strategic edge. We'll never know for certain, but something sparked the realization in Christine that he "gets it."

Yet, it wasn't vanity that dictated Matt's look. Far from being an overly polished figurehead, his visual appearance stemmed from self-assurance. His composed alertness set the stage. Standing tall and poised in the waiting area, he projected readiness and anticipation for the interview.

When Christine approached, Matt's smile was wide and authentic—a silent yet powerful introduction. He stepped forward, extending his hand first, ensuring a handshake that was confident and steady. Every micro-expression and gesture, from his steady eye contact to his assertive stance, communicated leadership. Those subtle cues, frequently unnoticed, were the threads

weaving a significant impression upon Christine. Matt's outward presentation reflected his internal preparedness, a synchrony that Christine keenly observed. It was the finesse that transformed a prospect into a serious candidate for the regional operations director role.

Matt aimed to present as successful but, more critically, he wanted to be recognized as someone who could seamlessly integrate into the agency's mission and uphold the high standards required of this leadership role. In fact, he hoped Christine would see past his appearance and acknowledge his potential to contribute meaningfully to leading strategic initiatives and advancing interagency collaboration. He aspired to render his appearance inconsequential, to be trusted immediately and seen as capable of excellence in guiding complex operations and inspiring confidence in his teams.

The Cost of a Poor Professional Identity

Perfection is unattainable, and everyone—you, me, and those in the highest echelons of the service and duty sector—is prone to missteps. Striving for flawless performance in every aspect of your professional identity is a noble goal, but it's important to recognize that occasional lapses are inevitable.

Some errors may go unnoticed, but others could become widely known. It could be a lapse in decorum at an official event, an inadvertently shared comment online about a sensitive issue that doesn't sit well publicly, or a day when your look of leadership might not meet the expected standards of your role. How you present yourself, how you dress, and how you carry yourself is constantly under scrutiny and can significantly influence perceptions. Not upholding the highest professional standards in every aspect of your work, including your visual presence, can result in significant consequences. Here are some of them:

Diminished credibility: A leader's visual presence plays a crucial role in shaping how they're perceived by their teams and the public. If their professional identity doesn't align with expected standards of authority and service, it can lead to doubts about their credibility and effectiveness in leading critical operations.

Loss of respect: When leaders don't consistently present themselves at their best, it can lead to a loss of respect from their teams and the public. This diminished respect can affect interactions and dynamics within units, agencies, or departments, impacting overall performance and morale.

Distraction from leadership objectives: An inconsistent professional identity can divert attention from a leader's strategic goals, such as implementing new policies, managing mission-critical operations, or fostering collaboration, hindering their primary focus on driving institutional success.

Stagnant career trajectory: A misalignment in professional identity can hinder a leader's chances for promotion or landing more significant roles within their agency or sector.

Operational and financial consequences: A professional identity that is not in sync with expectations can negatively influence public trust or agency effectiveness, directly affecting institutional outcomes, such as reduced funding, operational inefficiencies, or diminished public confidence.

Diminished earning potential: Perceived inconsistencies or errors in a leader's professional identity can hinder their ability to lead initiatives successfully, achieve recognition, or advance their careers, ultimately reducing their overall earning potential.

Undermining of professional boundaries: Inappropriate elements of a professional identity can blur the lines of professional boundaries, increasing the risk of misinterpretation or misconduct in interactions with teams or the public.

Public image risks: A lapse in professional identity can quickly become amplified in the media, social media, or public discourse, damaging the reputation of both the leader and their agency.

Do you think this sounds far-fetched? Think again. Yes, we all like to think about visual aspects as "superficial" factors, as something trivial or inconsequential. It's a topic many prefer to avoid or dismiss. Nevertheless, if we truly believed appearance didn't matter—and weren't acutely aware of its consequences—why would so many of us still find ourselves posing these questions?

- Do I need to invest in premium brands to create a professional identity that reflects the authority of my role?
- Is there a risk of going too far with an overly polished look coming across as out of touch with my team or the communities I serve?
- How formal is too formal for internal briefings or casual field meetings?
- Should I embrace a style that allows my personality to shine through while maintaining the polished look expected of a leader in service and duty?
- How much should I adapt my appearance to reflect my agency's mission and culture?
- Do I need to adjust my style based on whether I'm addressing senior leadership, collaborating with field teams in operational zones, or engaging with the public in town halls?
- Should I make an effort to appear more approachable and relatable, or lean into a more traditional, authoritarian look that reflects experience and rank?
- Does it even matter when many of my interactions with my team or the public are virtual?
- How can I avoid appearing disheveled after hours in the field or long travel days to regional offices?
- For informal gatherings with my team, where is the line between being relatable and appearing too casual?

- If I wear a uniform, how can I ensure it reflects the authority and professionalism of my role while remaining approachable?
- How do I balance individuality and authenticity while adhering to the uniform's strict standards?

Ever caught yourself ruminating on any of those questions? You're not alone.

Those are just a few of the underlying questions that cross many leaders' minds, whether occasionally or on a regular basis as they seek to balance the scales of authenticity and conformity within the expectations of the service and duty sector. Each choice is like a thread in the tapestry of our professional identity, woven together in the hopes of crafting a presence that resonates with both who we are and who we aspire to be in our careers.

Is there an easy answer to these questions?

Not exactly. There's no one-size-fits-all formula that can easily be applied to navigate this complexity, whether in person or online.

But you might be surprised that my recommendation is not to highlight your visual presence but to neutralize it. Your goal should be to ensure your visual presence neither detracts from you nor defines you. Instead, you want the spotlight on your expertise in strategic leadership, your contributions to mission success, and your ability to inspire trust and confidence in your teams and the public. Your appearance is about mastering the art of subtlety by making sure yours is neither a talking point nor a distraction. Your aim should be that your presence—your eloquence, acumen, and ability to lead effectively—commands the room (or your virtual engagements), not what you're wearing.

Of course, you also can decide at any time to make your visual presence the center of attention. In fact, it's something I constantly embrace.

If you've ever seen me on stage or watched footage from my engagements, you'll notice that I step out in the most elaborate, unique looks, from striking colors to architectural cuts, from bold

patterns to intricate designs, from avant-garde silhouettes to meticulously tailored ensembles. For my engagements I always aim to be the one who stands out, who draws eyes, who owns and captivates the room, even with my visual presence.

But remember, I'm on stage where all eyes are on me and, as a professional keynote speaker, my role is to captivate and engage my audience from the moment I step into the spotlight. It's also my responsibility to not only deliver compelling content but also to embody the principles of perception and visual presence that I advocate. I'm simply walking my talk, demonstrating firsthand the power of maintaining an intentionally crafted visual identity.

But in your day-to-day leadership, this is an approach you must handle with care. You want to ensure your expertise in operational leadership, your contributions to your agency's mission, and your ability to inspire confidence capture attention, making your visual presence an inconsequential backdrop rather than the focal point. You should strive to be memorable for your ability to lead your team and to drive outcomes, not your style. In the professional arena of service and duty, you want your achievements, insights, and leadership to shine, so your appearance should complement rather than overshadow your true value.

And yes, ideally your expertise should be the sole focus, but the very nature of being in leadership demands an exceptional ability to shape positive perceptions through your professional identity at all times. Leaders face unique challenges in this regard, encountering obstacles that those in non-leadership roles may not experience as intensely. These challenges can include the following:

High-stakes encounters: As a leader in service and duty, you frequently interact with senior leaders, interagency collaborators, or high-profile stakeholders who have elevated expectations. Meeting these demands requires maintaining a polished professional identity and consistently delivering value under pressure, whether it's handling a sensitive public inquiry, briefing senior officials on critical operations, or addressing concerns in a high-pressure meeting.

Professional identity is your product: You usually don't work directly in a role that demands selling a physical product or service, hence your individual perception is your product. It is intrinsically tied to the perceived value of what you're offering—yourself, your expertise, and your vision for fulfilling the mission of your agency. The "packaging" you present matters immensely in the service and duty sector where first impressions can significantly impact trust, collaboration, and confidence in your leadership.

Constantly being evaluated: You're perpetually being sized up by teams, senior leaders, and the public who are looking for any reasons to disqualify you. Your visual presence is a continuous data point being scrutinized—not just in formal meetings but also in informal interactions, public engagements, or even off-duty moments when your professional identity still reflects your role. Leadership presence in service and duty doesn't take breaks; it's a 24/7 commitment.

Representing the agency: As one of the faces of your agency, your professional identity reflects its values and standards while reinforcing its ethos and mission. It demonstrates a commitment to excellence that permeates the agency, from field operations to administrative offices. By embodying the principles of integrity, service, and dedication, you elevate the agency's reputation, building public trust and inspiring those under your leadership.

Overcoming preconceptions: Let's face it: There might be leaders within or even outside your agency who think, *I could manage this mission better,* or *I could lead this task force more effectively.* A colleague might think, *I could present this briefing more convincingly,* or a stakeholder might doubt your ability to deliver results. Hence, you must work harder to overcome any preexisting biases others have formed from your visible representation before getting the opportunity to prove your capabilities.

Emotionally charged environments: In service and duty, your role isn't just about executing tasks or achieving metrics. It's about serving communities, protecting lives, and fulfilling missions that often carry significant emotional stakes. Constituents look to you for reassurance, leadership, and solutions. Meeting or exceeding those expectations can build trust, loyalty, and confidence in your ability to lead effectively in high-pressure environments.

Cultural differences: Rarely do leaders in service and duty operate exclusively within a single cultural context. Your teams, partners, and the public come from diverse backgrounds, each with their own set of expectations. This diversity necessitates a nuanced understanding and adaptability to navigate cross-cultural interactions in today's interconnected world.

Digital identity: The leadership landscape is rapidly evolving with the increasing prominence of digital platforms. Leaders are now faced with the challenge of maintaining a digital identity that is under constant observation. Almost every day they engage in digital interactions, whether it's addressing public concerns online, managing their agency's social media presence, or conducting virtual meetings with teams or constituents. Your digital presence is as much a part of your professional identity as your in-person interactions.

Yet, this complexity is not a barrier but an invitation, an invitation to lead with intentionality, to craft a narrative that transcends superficial judgments and taps into the deeper currents of human connection and influence. Your professional identity is not just a veneer; it's a conduit through which your true leadership essence flows.

And in the end, the cost of a poor professional identity is not measured in missed promotions or failed salary raises. It's in your lost potential to make a meaningful impact, to leave a legacy that reflects not just what you did but how you made people feel. So as you move forward, let your professional identity be a reflection of the best version of you. Strive not for perfection but for intention.

Shaping Your Narrative with Intention

Every choice you make, every action you take, and every impression you leave must be driven by a clear and purposeful intent. As a leader in service and duty you cannot afford to leave your professional identity to chance. The stakes are too high and the ripple effects too profound on public trust, team performance, and institutional outcomes.

An intentional approach to your professional identity ensures you're not just reacting to the demands and expectations of those around you but proactively shaping the narrative of who you are and what you stand for. It helps you strip away the extraneous and focus on what truly matters in serving your mission. This conscious effort is what sets great service and duty leaders apart. It allows you to create a cohesive and compelling professional identity that resonates deeply with others, builds trust, and commands respect from your teams and the public.

When your actions are driven by clear intentions, you're not just influencing others' perceptions on a surface level, you're more likely to inspire confidence and loyalty among them. This is because teams and the public are drawn to leaders who have a clear sense of direction and demonstrate unwavering commitment to their mission.

So it's essential to be intentional in how you present yourself in every interaction, because doing so can have far-reaching effects. Whether you're engaging with community members, meeting with your teams, collaborating with colleagues, or representing your agency at public events, your professional identity extends beyond the immediate interaction. It shapes perceptions, builds trust, and enhances credibility—not just for you but for the agency or cause you represent. So now let's explore how your intentional identity reverberates across various aspects of your professional and personal lives.

Consider the impact on yourself. When you, as a leader, project confidence and competence through your professional identity, you're more likely to feel empowered and capable in your role. This self-assurance can translate directly into improved leadership performance, whether you're managing a critical operation or addressing public concerns during a crisis.

Reflect on your familial and social circle. The way you present yourself not only influences your own psyche but also extends to the perceptions of your family members, friends, and broader social networks. Upholding a professional identity can establish a halo of trust and respect that permeates your entire personal support system, reflecting the high standards you uphold in your professional life.

Think about those you interact with. Team members, senior leaders and the public—any of these individuals form their initial impressions of you based on various factors, including your visual presence. By consciously presenting yourself in the best possible way, you inspire trust and credibility, laying the groundwork for stronger relationships and better outcomes in mission success and institutional efficiency.

Recognize the impact on your team's reputation. Your professional identity doesn't just reflect on you, it significantly influences your team's reputation as well. Team members aspire to confidently say, "I work for [Your Name]" as a badge of credibility and prestige. When you represent yourself with excellence, you not only gain their trust but also empower them to leverage your association to enhance their own standing, reinforcing their professional identity.

Consider the ripple effect on your team. As a leader, the way you present yourself sets the tone and example for your entire team. Your professional identity provides team members with a model to emulate in mission-critical operations, public engagements, and everyday tasks. You can inspire your teams to raise

their own professional standards and follow your lead in fulfilling your agency's mission with excellence.

Acknowledge the agency you represent. Whether operating within a federal agency, a local government office, or a multinational task force, the way you uphold high standards casts a reflection, not just on you but on the agency you represent. Your professional identity reinforces the core values of your agency and inspires trust among team members and the public.

Think about future employers or partners. The professional identity you build now can open doors for career opportunities or strategic partnerships by preceding you before you even meet potential collaborators or senior leaders (or realize they're considering you for a new role or initiative).

Reflect on the sector as a whole. Beyond just your current role, the cumulative impact of leaders upholding the highest levels of excellence elevates societal perceptions of the service and duty sector overall. Your individual efforts contribute to greater respect and appreciation for the value that outstanding leadership provides.

Evaluate the institutional and public implications. Your individual leadership identity contributes to the collective perceptions of the agency or sector you serve. The way you present yourself sets a benchmark for professionalism and can influence public trust, team confidence, and the overall reputation of your sector.

Generational impact and legacy. The example you set through your professional identity helps shape the next generation of service and duty leaders. Your professional identity provides a benchmark for aspiring leaders to continuously raise the professional bar, ensuring a legacy of excellence for years to come.

Without intention, your professional identity is subject to the whims of external perceptions and circumstances. You may find yourself constantly reacting to the expectations of your team, senior leaders, or the public, struggling to maintain control over how you're perceived in the high-stakes service and duty sector.

This reactive stance can create a fragmented identity, making it difficult for others to discern who you are and what you represent as a leader in service and duty. Without intention, your actions might appear inconsistent, your decisions might lack alignment with your agency's mission, and your overall presence might come across as unstable. Teams, collaborators, and even the public may become unsure of what you stand for.

An unintentional professional identity not only confuses others but also erodes your own sense of purpose. It leaves you reactive instead of proactive, vulnerable to the shifting demands and perceptions of those around you. Over time, this lack of control can dilute your influence, hinder your credibility, and weaken your ability to lead effectively.

Intention doesn't take a break; it cannot go on leave or be set aside during downtime. It must be applied consistently, whether you're addressing your team in a command center, collaborating with interagency partners in a strategy session, briefing senior leaders on critical operations, or stepping into a public forum. It must extend through every single touchpoint, including those moments when it feels like no one is watching, because in service and duty, someone always is.

The Science of First Impressions

Let me introduce you to another study on first impressions that highlights the essential aspects of the research and its implications for our daily interactions. But remember, this is just one piece of the larger scientific puzzle, illustrating that, while first impressions can be powerful, their specific interpretations may vary based on context and individual circumstances.

Neuroscientists at NYU and Harvard, led by Elizabeth Phelps, identified the brain systems involved in forming first impressions. Their findings, reported in *Nature Neuroscience*, show how we encode and evaluate social information to make initial judgments.

Phelps' study was based on the idea that meeting someone new presents us with ambiguous and complex information—primarily visual but also involving other senses like hearing, smell, or touch. We quickly process this information to decide if we're attracted to the person or not.

This is a deeply ingrained process from our evolutionary past that helped our ancestors assess people as friends or foes, leaders or burdens. To understand this process researchers designed an experiment examining brain activity during initial evaluations of fictional individuals. Participants received written profiles of twenty individuals, each with different personality traits, and then they were shown pictures of those fictional people. The profiles included both positive (e.g., intelligent) and negative traits (e.g., lazy). Participants then rated how much they liked or disliked each individual based on the profiles. For example, if a participant valued intelligence highly and was less bothered by laziness, they might form a positive impression. While participants made these evaluations, researchers used functional magnetic resonance imaging (fMRI) to observe brain activity.

The study revealed significant activity in two brain regions during impression formation. The posterior cingulate cortex, associated with economic decision-making and assigning value to rewards, and the amygdala, linked to emotional learning and social evaluations based on trust or race group, were both highly active. Those areas were particularly engaged when encoding information that shaped the first impression. The findings suggest, even with brief encounters and limited cues, that our brains engage regions important in emotional learning and value representation. Those regions sort information based on personal significance and summarize it into a single value—a first impression. Essentially, our emotional learning plus our values equals the leader's imprint.

Here's how the principles from the study apply to leadership.

First impressions set the tone. As a leader in service and duty, the first impression you make sets the stage for how others perceive your competence, trustworthiness, and overall effectiveness in fulfilling your mission. Just as the study illustrates, your visual cues, and even the briefest interactions, can leave a lasting impression. It's essential to be mindful of these elements from the very first moment you engage with someone, whether it's a new team member, a key stakeholder, or a member of the public.

Emotional and value-based perception. The study also demonstrates that our brains use emotional learning and value-based assessment to form first impressions. For leaders in service and duty, this implies that your professional identity is not just about the qualities you project but also about how others interpret those qualities. Your actions, expressions, and demeanor need to resonate with the values and emotional states of those you interact with, aligning with the sector's emphasis on trust, integrity, and service.

The power of visual cues. The amygdala's role in processing visual information highlights the importance of visual cues in forming impressions. For leaders, this means paying attention to the nonverbal elements of your professional identity, even before you speak. Your appearance, body language, and demeanor in briefings, public forums, or operational settings can significantly impact how you're perceived by teams and the public.

Strategic use of first impressions. Leaders in service and duty can strategically use first impressions to their advantage. By consciously crafting your first impression to align with the values and expectations of those you serve, you can create an instantly powerful and persuasive presence that embodies the principles of service, integrity, and leadership.

Now let's step away from the academic deep dive and move into something a bit more practical. Imagine this: I hand you a list of twenty random items to memorize. After a while I ask you to recall them. Which ones do you think you're most likely to remember? If you're like most people, it's the first and the last items on the list that stick in your memory.

Here's why: Our incredibly energy-efficient brain is made up of around one hundred billion neurons. That's lots of brain cells needing fuel to keep us ticking. Think of our brain like our smartphone or laptop. When the battery is running low in our device, what happens? The screen dims, nonessential functions shut down, and the device goes into low-power mode to conserve energy until we can recharge it.

Likewise, our brain, aiming to conserve energy, prioritizes what it processes and remembers. This is why the first and last items on a list—the ones our brain encounters first and last—are most often remembered. It's an efficient way to save energy while still holding onto critical pieces of information.

Or how often have you heard that, when giving a presentation, the introduction and conclusion should be the most compelling parts? Same principle. Starting with a strong hook and ending with a powerful last statement ensures your message resonates long after you've finished speaking. Or think about crafting an email about a mission update to your team when we often spend more time perfecting the subject line or the opening sentence to grab the recipient's attention than on any other part of the message. And then there's the closing line that wraps everything up neatly. Again, it's the same principle.

So what does this mean for your professional identity as a leader? It underscores the importance of making a strong first impression and leaving a memorable lasting impression. The brain's tendency to remember the beginning and end more vividly than the middle means your initial interaction and your closing moments are crucial, or at least they will flavor how everything in the middle is perceived.

As leaders we need to harness this understanding to ensure the key messages and impressions we want to leave are clearly conveyed at the start and end of our interactions, whether we're addressing teams, briefing senior leaders, or representing our agency at public events.

The Sustained Imprint

Make no mistake—don't think your image is dependent solely on those first micro-moments, and the rest doesn't matter. Your professional identity is deepened by much more; it's an ongoing process. Yes, your initial impression is pivotal, yet it's merely the precursor to what must become a deeply rooted perception. Consider this the inception of your "sustained imprint."

It's the ongoing cultivation of this first impression that cements your professional identity and maintains its potency over time. Without nurturing, even the most stellar beginnings can fade, losing their resonance and diminishing their initial influence.

I once developed and organized a leadership seminar for a group of leaders I worked with in Europe. The participants were surprised to discover that their trainer was not a person; instead, we trained them with the help of horses.

In one of the first exercises we split the participants into two groups. The first group went into the riding area where an unleashed horse was waiting for them.

The participants were told to walk straight in with confident steps, to appear strong, to keep eye contact with the horse, and to keep a straight face. When they arrived at the horse they had to smack their horsewhips on the ground several times. The horse immediately began to run in a circle. The participants whipped and whipped, and they were briefed to stop when the horse appeared to be tired or ready for the next step.

When they put aside the whip, something magical happened: The horse followed them everywhere. Participants walked around the arena, and their assigned horse happily trotted after them.

None of the participants had said one word to the horse. The horse just followed.

The second group received a different briefing. They were supposed to walk in and appear friendly and kind to the horse. They were told to motivate the horse by petting it, talking to it, and developing a relationship with it. They even brought in treats and encouraged the horse with all their hearts.

The first observation we made was that they had a really hard time making the horse run in a circle. It was obvious the horse wanted more treats and more tender loving care. Not much happened. The horse didn't follow them and, at one point, it didn't even come back for more treats because, obviously, there were no more.

What did we learn? Horses, much like humans, respond to the nonverbal cues of confidence and assertiveness. The first group's authoritative approach, conveyed through their posture, gaze, and decisive actions, left a compelling imprint on the horses, commanding respect and prompting a clear behavioral response.

This underscores the power of making a strong initial imprint. Without uttering a single word, the first group's commanding conduct set the tone for the interaction, resulting in the horses' compliance and subsequent allegiance.

We also learned that being liked is not the ultimate goal of leadership; instead, being respected is. As a leader, it's crucial to understand that respect is the foundation upon which effective leadership is built. Being liked is a bonus.

But that doesn't mean you should start wielding a metaphorical whip with your team. Leadership is not about instilling fear or using intimidation. It's about inspiring others through your actions and your unwavering commitment to excellence. It's about creating a culture of mutual respect where everyone is encouraged to bring their best selves to the table and work toward a common mission. Leadership is not about force; it's about influence.

But throughout the next days of our leadership event, we also observed that the first horse group, emboldened by their initial success, celebrated with a sense of triumph, embodying the spirit

of leadership and victory. But as time progressed, the complexity of their challenge unfolded. They began to display inconsistency in their conduct and actions. To the horse, their once clear and commanding presence became unpredictable. And predictability, consistency, is the cornerstone of leadership; it's what engenders trust and respect. The first group, although initially successful in commanding attention, failed to uphold the robustness of that initial imprint. They did not succeed in cultivating it into a sustained imprint. The horses' diminishing responses were a clear testament to the group's faltering consistency.

The lesson was vivid and unequivocal: A leader's impact is measured not only by the strength of their initial imprint but also by the presence they sustain over time. The game isn't over after seven (or whatever) seconds. Outstanding leaders in service and duty leave lasting impressions by how they consistently present themselves, always and everywhere.

Like Evan's experience, the positive imprint developed in mere seconds only got him in the door. It made the possibility of acceptance real. It broke down the barrier between him and Christine. But the true test of his professional identity will be in how he sustains and builds upon that initial approval, demonstrating his value and substance in every subsequent interaction and decision in the near future and beyond.

Conversely, the negative impression that Matt created caused the door to slam shut. It reduced the possibility of acceptance and created a barrier between him and the person he met who, in this case, had the power to either help him up the ladder of success or pass him by in favor of someone else. He will never get the chance to prove his excellence or reveal the depth of his expertise because the brief encounter in the waiting area cast a shadow over his interview.

In every setting that calls for your close attention, every interaction contributes to your lasting professional identity, even moments when you aren't paying close attention. That's because, truth be told, most of the day we run on autopilot, not recognizing that we're under constant observation.

I illustrate this in my keynotes by asking participants to take a selfie. As they excitedly prepare to capture their picture-perfect portrait, employing what digital culture has taught us—to position their face and body perfectly, to smile, to raise an eyebrow—I interrupt them with a seemingly impossible challenge: no posing, no adjusting their hair, no putting on their best "camera-ready" face, no tilting the head to find the most flattering angle, no sucking in the stomach or pushing out the chest, no last-minute adjustments to clothing or accessories.

Just take a raw, unfiltered snapshot of themselves at that exact moment. The result is a revelation, a picture that showcases how they're observed by others most of the day when they forget about their environments, forget they're always on stage, forget that someone's always watching. It's a stark contrast to the carefully curated images we often present to the world, a reminder that our true selves are not always the polished versions we'd like to portray.

This simple exercise is a powerful testament to the fact that our professional identity is not just crafted in the moments we're acutely aware of but in the everyday instances when we let our guard down. It's in those unguarded moments that our real selves shine through, and it's those genuine glimpses that can leave the most lasting impressions on those around us.

Imagine sitting at your desk during a quiet moment, engrossed in catching up on emails, thinking you're alone. You may not see it as a formal leadership moment, but as team members walk by, they notice how you carry yourself in those unguarded moments. Are you approachable, focused, and calm, or do you appear tense, disengaged, or frustrated? Or picture yourself in the aisles of a grocery store, picking up a few items on the way home. Without realizing it, a colleague recognizes you. The way you interact with the cashier, react to a minor inconvenience, or handle a quick exchange with someone in line may leave an impression—positive or negative—on those who see you, even if you don't see them. Think about waiting in line at a coffee shop or sitting in a public space between meetings.

You may believe it's a moment to unwind or catch your breath, but those around you, including members of the public, may be observing your posture, expressions, or even your tone in a brief phone call.

In all these scenarios your actions, tone, and demeanor—whether intentional or habitual—contribute to the sustained imprint you leave as a leader. These seemingly insignificant moments are often the ones that stick with people the longest, shaping their perception of your character and reinforcing your professional identity.

The Invisible Filters of Perception

For just a moment, put yourself in the shoes of a patient. You find yourself needing quick medical care and, as you enter a doctor's practice, a sea of expectations and anxieties floods your mind. The receptionist is busy typing, not noticing you right away. As seconds tick by—which seem like an eternity—you start to feel ignored.

During that time your eyes wander, and you can't help but notice the receptionist's nails look like they could use some attention. Their makeup and hair seem a bit much for such an early hour. When they finally do greet you, your patience has worn thin. You were on time, but now they've left you waiting. Finally, sitting in the waiting room you spot a crumpled piece of paper under a chair, missed by the cleaners, perhaps. The chairs around you show signs of age with cracks and worn edges. Then, as you're finally called to see the doctor, a strange smell drifts from the staff room. Maybe they just had lunch?

The doctor comes to get you, moving quickly, not stopping for introductions or handshakes. Their shoes have seen better days, and their white coat has lost some of its brightness. All these little things add up in your mind, painting a picture of a place that might not be up to the mark. *No wonder*, you think. *This seems to be the standard in this practice*—a standard that feels lacking.

What you experienced is the powerful influence of unconscious biases. The sights and impressions, from the receptionist's appearance to the subtle cues of the environment, all funnel through your perceptions, coloring your expectations, possibly without a word being spoken. Unconscious biases are mental shortcuts or patterns of thinking that influence perceptions without conscious awareness. These biases often stem from deeply embedded social stereotypes, personal experiences, or prevailing cultural norms.

Let me share a personal anecdote that also illuminates how a variety of biases can work against us, even in the most intimate of settings. I'm married to a German mathematician and engineer who works in finance and IT. Let's indulge in a few stereotypes about Germans for a moment. In his life everything must be sorted and organized in a particular way. He thrives on order and structure. My cultural background, on the other hand, is Mediterranean, which comes with a relaxed approach to life, embracing its fullness and finding joy in daily adventures that aren't always meticulously structured or planned.

Picture this: I'm the wife who goes to the refrigerator, takes out a bottle of sparkling water, and puts it back without securing the cap as tightly as my German husband would expect. And that often leads to one of those minor arguments that anyone in a relationship is probably familiar with. But here's the interesting part—he finds every single item I leave open in our home, and I mean e.v.e.r.y.t.h.i.n.g. But he never seems to register the things I do close and, believe me, I do close things.

What's at play here is a medley of biases working against me. His brain embarks on a journey, subconsciously seeking evidence to shape his perception of me in a particular way. He might think, *She's always leaving things open*, or *She's not as organized as I am*. But the reality is far more nuanced. It's not that I never close things; it's just that his mind is attuned to noticing the instances that confirm his preconceived notions.

The same is true for your teams and constituents.

Their minds go on journeys too, shaping their perceptions based on a complex interplay of biases and preconceptions. They might fixate on a single interaction or characteristic that confirms their existing beliefs while overlooking the multitude of instances that contradict it.

As a leader, recognizing and navigating these biases is crucial. It's not about striving for perfection or trying to control every perception. Rather, it's about understanding that these biases exist and consistently presenting your best self in a way that invites others to see beyond their initial assumptions. It's about building a professional identity that, over time, paints a comprehensive picture of your leadership.

Imagine one of your team members arriving for a critical briefing about a high-stakes operation or community initiative. If your workspace appears disorganized with files scattered or an environment that seems chaotic, it could unintentionally signal a lack of professionalism or preparedness on your part. Your team may start questioning your attention to detail before you even begin the discussion. Or consider encountering a member of the public during a community event. If you greet them looking flustered or distracted, their unconscious minds may leap to conclusions about your ability to stay composed under pressure or effectively lead in moments that demand public trust and confidence.

The impactful takeaway is that we all innately make subconscious assessments that are further influenced by our unconscious biases. These biases are like silent storytellers, weaving narratives that may not be accurate or fair but that, nonetheless, shape interactions and decisions in profound ways.

Confirmation bias is one of the most prominent unconscious biases. Confirmation bias is a psychological phenomenon in which individuals favor information that confirms their preexisting beliefs or hypotheses. It's the tendency to seek information that validates their existing perceptions. This means we're more likely to notice details that support what we already think, often overlooking evidence to the contrary.

From the moment you walked through the door of the doctor's practice, your brain was picking up on cues and details that combined to form an impression. When the receptionist didn't immediately look up, their unpolished appearance confirmed any lurking thoughts that the practice was disorganized. Each subsequent observation, from the crumpled paper to the worn furniture to the doctor's hurried entrance, built upon this initial judgment. Instead of seeing these as isolated instances, confirmation bias led you to interpret them as part of a pattern, reinforcing the belief that the practice did not meet the standards of care you expected. Each detail seemed to confirm your initial impression, and this bias can be challenging to overcome once it takes root.

Anchoring bias is another pervasive mental shortcut we often take in which we rely too heavily on the first piece of information we receive—the anchor—and allow it to disproportionately influence our subsequent decisions. Once an anchor is set, other interpretations and information, even if more relevant or factual, tend to be viewed through the lens of this initial reference point.

Suppose the initial delay and the receptionist's disheveled appearance were the first bits of information you registered. These details likely became your anchor. As you continued to wait, even before noticing the crumpled paper or the smell from the staff room, your mind was already anchored to the notion that this practice was subpar. This early anchor had an impact on your entire perception of the care provided, regardless of the actual quality of the medical services you received.

The horn effect leads you to attribute negative characteristics based on a single perceived flaw, causing you to view all traits of an individual or entity negatively. For example, the receptionist's posture, which could be neutral or simply a product of a long day, might seem to you to indicate a lack of interest or enthusiasm. This bias can lead you to overlook any instances of competence or moments of kindness as you focus instead on the traits that seem to confirm your initial negative impression.

Negativity bias is another cognitive phenomenon in which negative aspects have a more significant impact on an individual's psychological state than do neutral or positive ones. Essentially, we tend to pay more attention to negative experiences or information. Did you notice the receptionist's meticulous uniform? Or what about the effort they put into carefully documenting patient cases, a sign of thoroughness and dedication? Did you observe the efficiency with which they eventually handled your paperwork or the accuracy in their data entry? Similarly, the doctor's speed may have been a reflection of their ability to manage a busy practice effectively, ensuring every patient receives timely care. But those positive traits may have been eclipsed by the more immediate negative judgments, steering your overall impression toward the unfavorable due to negativity bias.

Selection bias further forces your mind to focus on every little flaw. You notice the tiniest speck of dirt, a slight tear in the curtain, or a faint noise from the air conditioner. You continue to selectively pick out all the negatives while ignoring anything positive about the experience.

Self-serving bias might come into play when you think, *I always pick the wrong practice*, making you feel even more justified in your negative assessment. This bias reinforces the idea that the problem lies with the practice, not with any external factors or mere chance.

The illusion of control makes you feel like you could have avoided a bad experience if only you had chosen a different practice. You think you had control over the situation, and this misplaced belief adds to your frustration because you believe you should have foreseen and avoided the negative aspects.

And even after you've left the practice, unconscious biases continue to steer your mind.

Availability bias, for example, ensures you overestimate the importance of certain events or outcomes based on their ease of recall. This means the negative aspects you noticed loom larger in your memory than the positive ones. Those negatives become the ready examples that come to mind when you reflect on your visit or discuss it with others. This tendency can extend to the point where you might find yourself browsing online reviews of the practice, unconsciously searching for confirmation of your initial opinion. As you skim through numerous positive testimonials, they barely register; instead, your attention zeroes in on the few critical remarks. These resonate with your experience, reinforcing your perspective. Feeling validated, you consider it almost a duty to add your own critique.

The bandwagon effect is a bias that compels us to adopt beliefs or behaviors because they seem popular or because others are doing it. In this context, the critical comments of others echo your own impressions, and the weight of collective criticism may feel like undeniable proof, further solidifying your initial judgments.

The Dunning-Kruger effect also may take hold as you consider leaving a review. Feeling qualified to evaluate the entire medical staff after a single visit, this bias overstates your own expertise, leading you to assert judgments that might not reflect the true caliber of the healthcare professionals' skills and services.

The sunk cost fallacy may cause you to persist in viewing the practice negatively because you've already invested in visits and treatments there, despite there being evidence of good care in the future.

I could go on and on. After all, at the moment of writing this book, science is aware of approximately 185 biases that influence the human mind. These biases work beneath the surface of consciousness and affect every aspect of our lives, from the mundane to the critical, without us even realizing it.

Understanding these biases is key to navigating the complex landscape of human thought and perception, allowing us to make more informed and deliberate choices. And although unconscious biases can have a harmful effect by manifesting in serious issues like workplace harassment and obstructing diversity efforts, they also can play a positive role for you in the brief window in which perceptions are formed. In this narrow but critical time frame, you can harness the power of these biases to your advantage.

By being aware of them and intentionally presenting yourself in a manner that aligns positively from the very first moments, you can influence others to see you in a more favorable light. This doesn't mean manipulating perceptions dishonestly but rather ensuring the genuine and best aspects of your professional identity are what shine through and resonate the most.

For the practice we just visited if, upon your arrival, the receptionist had briefly looked up and acknowledged you with a smile, making it clear they were wrapping up important work for another patient's care, your impression might have been different. Maybe they could have offered you a glass of water or a cup of coffee while you waited. Their unkempt nails might have faded into the background, overshadowed by their meticulous uniform and the courtesy of their instant greeting. You might have thought, *They're really dedicated to each patient's privacy and care.*

As you took your seat the receptionist's professionalism might have cast a positive light on the surroundings, making the waiting room's imperfections seem less significant. You might have noticed the beautiful paintings by a local artist instead of the torn curtain. When the doctor arrived promptly, their efficient manner could have been interpreted as a sign of a well-run practice that values a patient's time, turning a potentially negative first impression into a positive reflection of the practice's standards.

Now let's translate these insights into the world of leadership within the service and duty sector. Just as a patient's perception of a medical practice can be swayed by subtle cues and unconscious biases, your professional identity is shaped by countless factors, many of which you may not be aware of.

Consider an official walking into your office for a discussion about operational improvements or public initiatives. From the moment they step through the door, their mind is processing visual information and forming judgments. Is your workspace organized and reflective of the agency's mission? Does your office convey professionalism with up-to-date materials and branding that align with the agency's values? Are the documents on your desk neatly arranged and accessible? Do you appear prepared and composed, radiating confidence and a readiness to tackle critical challenges?

Each of these visual elements contributes to the overall impression of you as a leader. As the meeting progresses, they will continue to assess you based on a range of factors, from your demeanor and body language to your communication style and expertise. Any perceived flaw, such as a lack of clarity in your objectives, inconsistent follow-up on prior discussions, or even a momentary pause when answering a question can trigger biases like the horn effect, causing the official to view your performance through a more critical lens. Anchoring bias will ensure they hold onto that first impression, whether positive or negative, and selection bias might drive them to zero in on every perceived flaw while filtering out the positives.

Imagine a team member observing their leader during a field visit. If the leader appears disengaged or inattentive to the team's immediate challenges, the team member might subconsciously question the leader's commitment to the mission, even if the leader ultimately addresses the situation effectively. This perception could linger, influencing the team member's trust in future scenarios. Or consider constituents at a service counter seeking assistance. If the front-line representative seems preoccupied or indifferent, the constituents might assume this reflects a broader inefficiency within the agency. They may start noticing other flaws, like outdated informational brochures or a less-than-welcoming waiting area, even if these are minor in the grand scheme. These initial impressions can shape their perception of the entire experience, even if their issue is ultimately resolved.

Unconscious biases extend far beyond the immediate moment. Only by understanding and being mindful of these biases can you take proactive steps to ensure your actions, demeanor, and environment project the positive, authoritative image you want to convey.

But it's not just about avoiding negative perceptions; it's about actively crafting positive ones. By consistently exceeding expectations and demonstrating excellence, you can leverage unconscious biases to work in your favor. This effort isn't about being average, it's about being remarkable, creating moments that resonate, inspire, and elevate. The question, then, isn't simply about avoiding pitfalls, it's about becoming unforgettable. How can you stand out as a leader in service and duty? The answer lies not only in what you do but in how you do it—with intention, with authenticity, and with a commitment to excellence in every action, every decision, and every interaction.

Standing Out for the Right Reasons

In the field of service and duty, where stakes are high and distinction is paramount, standing out is more than a personal goal, it's a professional necessity. Excellence is the new norm. Leaders aiming to succeed in this sector must transcend the ordinary. The truth is, "good" doesn't cut it anymore. Good is the baseline, the expectation. To be perceived as a leader—and to make a positive impact—you can't afford to simply fit the mold. Average blends in and, by blending in, you become invisible in the vast network of agencies, departments, or units.

Think of the game Tetris. For some readers, Tetris is a nostalgic nod to the past, a digital relic from the days of clunky, handheld gaming devices. For others, perhaps of a younger generation, it's a classic that's been rediscovered on smartphones and modern gaming platforms. No matter the version you're familiar with, the metaphor stands: Each piece that falls is designed to fit perfectly into a space, completing a line. The goal is to rotate and align falling blocks to complete lines.

But what happens when the line is completed? It disappears. This is a triumph in Tetris, but in your career within service and duty, it's a warning. When you align too perfectly with the patterns already in play, you risk becoming part of the background, another completed line that serves its purpose and then vanishes into the sea of sameness.

When leaders stand out they do so by transcending the ordinary. They become the piece in Tetris that not only fits but also starts a reaction, changing the landscape, challenging the status quo, and bringing new possibilities into play.

Standing out means being the architect of your perception, crafting your professional identity with intention, and making choices so that how you're viewed in the professional sphere will set you apart. It's about proactive distinction, carving out a space where your individuality and unique approach to your professional identity resonate unmistakably. This approach requires being the memorable piece that doesn't just fill a gap but also creates a new path for others to follow in improving public trust, operational efficiency, or community engagement.

You might be thinking, *Well, is it always good to stand out?*

For a pop star, standing out from the crowd in any way they can always results in a positive impact. Whatever gets their name in the press helps sell their music. For an entertainer, standing out from the crowd, regardless of the reason, is also good to an extent. If they appear on the evening news because they've done something out of order, they've still won the game. Or think of my personal example again when I'm the one on stage or working an audience, and it's crucial that I stand out to captivate and engage.

But in the professional universe of service and duty, standing out for its own sake is a terrible idea. In this space there's a great way to stand out, and there's a bad way to stand out. The surest path to standing out in the best way is to consistently do the following three things:

First, be your best self, bringing your unique personality to the forefront and cultivating a professional identity that highlights your individuality while aligning with the mission of service and public good.

Second, embody and uphold the highest values of your agency, serving as a living testament to its mission and principles and ensuring your professional identity reflects the integrity and values your team stands for.

And third, don't just meet expectations, surpass them, striving to go above and beyond what's anticipated in service delivery, team leadership, or community impact, and developing a professional identity that is synonymous with excellence.

The bad way to stand out is . . . well, any other way.

Let's say you walk into that doctor's practice again, except this time you're greeted not just by a friendly receptionist but also by a wave of innovation. The receptionist, with a welcoming nod, directs you to an interactive kiosk. It's an engaging check-in experience where you can personalize your visit, choosing room ambience settings from temperature to lighting to the background music. In the waiting area you're immersed in an environment designed for comfort and education. You instantly notice a refreshment bar, a gesture of hospitality that goes beyond the expected. The receptionist offers a selection of herbal teas and nutritious snacks, transforming the waiting time into a moment of relaxation and nourishment for body and mind.

In your hands a tablet becomes a window to new knowledge. With an augmented reality application you explore health topics in a way that's interactive, immersive, and personalized to your health journey. Posters on the wall spring to life, providing a depth of understanding that pamphlets could never match. Amidst all this a subtle scent fills the air. The receptionist explains it's aromatherapy, intentionally chosen to create an atmosphere of calm.

It's a thoughtful touch that eases the inherent tension of waiting for a medical appointment. Instead of outdated magazines, the area features an exhibition of local artists' works. The space is transformed into a sanctuary that indulges your senses and promotes healing.

At every turn this practice has gone above and beyond. Even feedback is revolutionized. With a real-time device you can express your level of satisfaction, empowering you as a partner in the care experience. Later in the day the doctor personally calls to check on your progress instead of delegating the task to administrative staff or software. This practice has redefined what it means to stand out, ensuring that, from the moment you walk in to the last farewell, your experience is anything but average.

As a leader duty, you too must reimagine what it means to stand out through your professional identity and leadership presence. Your visual presence is a powerful tool that can enhance your professional identity and create memorable connections with your teams and the public. Conversely, if not managed with intention and consistency, your visual presence can undermine your credibility and diminish the respect you command.

But standing out in service and duty isn't about making grand, exuberant changes. It's about the many small details that collectively create a powerful professional identity. It's not about being the loudest or most flamboyant; it's about being the most refined, consistent, and impactful in driving team performance, building trust, and delivering service that exceeds public expectations.

When Details Speak Loudest

In a world brimming with competence and competition, where "good" has become the standard, the nuances of excellence whisper the secrets of distinction. The fine print and subtleties can amplify your professional identity above a symphony of sameness because paying attention to detail speaks volumes.

It's the crisp dress uniform or the perfectly tailored suit that projects authority in a government office, the signature accessory that hints at creativity in public outreach events, or the elegantly simple briefcase that showcases your work with sophistication in a public service meeting. It's the polished shoes, subtly gleaming from beneath a conference table, that hint at a refined and thoughtful choice. It's the well-kept notebook with its neatly aligned edges, whispering of your methodical approach to policy discussions or strategic planning sessions. It's the gentle click of a quality pen, the unspoken ally of your thoughts during team briefings, and the smartwatch that discreetly keeps you on schedule in the fast-paced environment of public service. It's the website photograph that captures you engaged in a dynamic team briefing that sends a powerful message of collaboration. Or it's the professional headshot on your LinkedIn profile that speaks volumes about how seriously you take your leadership role.

Your professional identity is like a puzzle, each piece playing a crucial role in creating a complete and cohesive narrative of public service excellence. Every detail is a vital part of the whole. When every piece is thoughtfully placed, you build a powerful and memorable professional identity. Yet just as a puzzle with missing pieces is incomplete, neglecting any aspect of your professional identity can leave your narrative fragmented and less impactful.

In this puzzle no piece is too small, and no piece is insignificant. Rather, these nuances collectively weave the narrative of a leader's commitment to their field and their inherent role as a trailblazer.

In my keynotes I often illustrate how details can significantly influence judgments by sharing a fascinating video based on an actual study. The research involves twins who are dressed identically for various professional settings, such as two police officers, two managers, or two doctors. They sit side by side, looking alike in every way, except for a single crucial difference: One is chewing gum. Participants are seated in front of the twins and asked a series of questions: "Which one would be more likely to give you a parking ticket?" or "Which one would be more inclined to give you a raise or fire you if you asked for one?"

The questions delve deeper into the twins' perceived social lives with participants speculating about which twin is invited to more parties or has more friends. Even their supposed sex lives come under scrutiny. Surprisingly, perhaps, most individuals favor the gum-chewing twin across all of these scenarios. The presence of that seemingly insignificant detail—the act of chewing gum—is enough to sway perceptions and create an entirely different narrative around each twin.

Of course, in reality the relationship between a detail and these various outcomes is seldom so simple. Nevertheless, the study, which was later used in a video ad for a chewing gum brand, provides a compelling illustration of how easily our perceptions can be influenced by minor, often irrelevant factors.

For leaders, it serves as a powerful reminder of the need to be mindful and in control of the subtle details that can shape others' perceptions of us, sometimes in ways we might not anticipate or intend, thus underscoring the importance of being intentional about every aspect of our professional identity.

In the same vein, it's the finer details of presentation that can cause professionals in service and duty to stand out—and be remembered—for less favorable reasons, be it the overly casual hairstyle that might be perceived as too laid-back for a high-stakes meeting with policy advisors; a palette of colors more befitting of a fashion runway than a formal hearing; the jewelry that clinks and clatters distractingly during presentations; a bold fashion statement that might overshadow the substance of a pitch to a legislative committee; a shirt buttoned improperly, which can seem careless; a tie that's a bit too loud and may override professionalism in deference to fashion in a budget review session; an overpowering cologne that might be off-putting; or a laptop covered in an array of personal stickers that could undermine the organized professional identity you aim to project in a strategic planning meeting. All such details, no matter how insignificant they may seem, could overshadow your expertise and intent and inadvertently shift the focus away from your professional contributions as a leader.

These memorable yet incongruent details can lead others to remember you, not for your strategic acumen, but for your sartorial choices. Some may think, *Ah, yes, that's the community director with the rainbow-colored hair,* or *Sure, I remember those neon glasses, but I don't recall their name or their ideas.* Such details, even potentially irrelevant ones, have the potential to cast a long shadow, sometimes causing the positive aspects of your leadership to fade from memory.

Is this fair? Certainly not. But humans are built to think this way—including you and me.

Let's go back to another experience in a medical practice. Decades ago I needed a physical therapist to treat my back pain. At that time the internet was still a distant dream, and I recall the quaint process of selecting a practitioner based solely on insurance coverage and the luck of the draw in a paper telephone directory. Yes, I know, this dates me. Some of you might not even remember a time before Google.

Anyway, at my appointment I stumbled into a place that felt more like someone's home than a clinic. I navigated through a cluttered living room adorned with an eclectic assortment of plants, art, and odd collections—a creative chaos. Finally, I arrived at the treatment room. It was painted in sterile mint green and housed one of those physical therapy treatment tables enveloped in disposable paper.

And on that paper, which I thought was used for hygienic reasons, my eyes swiftly caught an unexpected sight: the remnants of a chicken bone! You read that right. Despite my initial shock—and I wish I could say I left instantly—I found myself discreetly disposing of the bone in the therapist's trash can. Moments later the therapist entered with a friendly greeting, apologizing for his absence due to a quick lunch break between patients.

I don't remember much about the treatment itself. To be fair, it might have been wonderful, his medical analysis might have been on point, and his treatment plan might have made sense. He might have shown genuine concern for my condition, offered insightful advice, and demonstrated remarkable skill.

Perhaps he even went above and beyond, providing a tailored exercise regimen or following up with a call to check on my progress. I don't remember how much I paid or how convenient the location was. All that lingers is the image of that chicken bone.

Did I ever return? No.

Have you ever walked into a department office for a policy briefing only to be subtly irritated by a team member's overly casual attire, a small rebellion against the formality expected in government meetings? Or perhaps you've sat in a colleague's workspace, noticing the scattered paperwork or leftover coffee cups, each item silently questioning their ability to manage tasks with precision? Think back to a trainer at a professional development seminar whose insights into compliance measures were momentarily overshadowed by typos in their presentation slides. Or the agency representative who delivered an impressive briefing but whose cluttered vehicle told a story of disorganization.

The bottom line is that one incongruent visual detail can distract from the core value you offer, even if just for a split second. But in the world of leadership, one second of doubt is an eternity.

If you think this is far-fetched, please think again. Take a look at the environments you work in and consider how much thought has been put into every visual detail. Public offices are designed to convey professionalism with standardized layouts and displays of achievements or institutional values. Meeting rooms are carefully arranged to encourage focus and collaboration, often adorned with institutional emblems or national symbols that emphasize mission-driven work. Fleet vehicles, representing your agency in the field, are maintained to ensure a professional exterior. Even the uniforms or dress codes followed by your team convey a deliberate message of authority and respect.

This necessity for attention to detail is not just true for the settings you manage but also for you personally and, by extension, for your teams, the individuals who operate in these environments. The same meticulousness applied to creating a positive public impression should be reflected in personal presentation and interactions, reinforcing the overall perception of excellence.

Successful leaders in service and duty understand and accept that everything is rooted in the details. The tiniest details can make us stand out, either positively or negatively. In a sea of sameness, where many leaders blend into the background, these details can become your secret weapons in building trust, credibility, and high-performing teams.

Embrace the power of nuance and use it to your advantage. And always remember that it's not about perfection, it's about intention. It's about making a conscious effort to present your best self in every interaction, no matter how small, whether you're addressing teams or representing your agency at public events.

Chapter 2
Your Professional Identity

The Indelible Mark
Etched in Others' Minds.

Chapter 2: Your Professional Identity

Let's begin with some clarity on the lingo. Terms abound in the "professional identity" context. Some might refer to it as "executive presence" or "professional image." Others might use "professional persona," and there are those who speak of "personal branding." Each term, although distinct, converges on a core principle—the essence of how you present, position, and define yourself.

I choose to call it professional identity because it encompasses more than just the surface level of your professional life. Unlike executive presence or professional image, which can imply a focus on outward appearance, professional identity digs deeper. It's the integration of your values, skills, experiences, and personal traits into a cohesive whole that defines you as a leader in service and duty—not just your look. It's a holistic approach that considers every facet of your professional existence, from your appearance and behavior to your communication, digital footprint, and the environment you create around you. It's this comprehensive nature that makes professional identity the most fitting term to describe the multifaceted and deeply personal nature of how we navigate our professional lives.

Our professional identity is a direct reflection of the attention and care we invest in our most valuable asset: ourselves. Each detail is a thread in the fabric of the impression we weave, not only benefiting our self-image but also enhancing the esteem of the agencies or institutions we represent.

The reputation of any agency—a government body, a regulatory commission, a public safety department, a community service entity—is significantly influenced by the professional identities of its representatives. And this is particularly true for leaders. As the direct link between their agency and their teams, they are often the first point of contact and play a crucial role in shaping perceptions of both the team's capabilities and the agency's credibility. Their professional identity can either reinforce their agency's mission or undermine it, making their conduct pivotal in establishing and maintaining public trust and effectiveness.

Although the story of Matt and Evan unfolded in an interview context, the essence of the so-called seven-second rule is universal. Whether you're stepping into a high-stakes team meeting about community initiatives, engaging in a virtual conference with regional partners, posting updates on social media about your agency's latest accomplishments, presenting a proposal for a grant or funding initiative, or attending an event in your community, your professional identity is established almost instantly. Changing this first imprint once it's formed is notoriously difficult. As you already know, once they're formed, perceptions become a filter through which all subsequent interactions are assessed.

For example, when Christine initially encountered Matt and unconsciously placed him in the "not suitable" category for the leadership role, changing that snap judgment was nearly impossible. Because said snap judgment was rooted in Christine's cognitive framework, it subconsciously forced her to seek information that reinforced her initial perceptions while ignoring evidence to the contrary. Matt's chance to make a positive impact on agency initiatives was lost before it began. On the flip side, when Christine met Evan, his professional presentation immediately pegged him as credible and competent in driving operational excellence and team morale. Christine's swift categorization was governed by the same cognitive processes that shaped her earlier judgment. Subconsciously, her brain was compelled to confirm her initial favorable impression, scanning for evidence to support Evan's suitability for the role.

In this subtle dance of cognition, Christine's brain worked diligently, albeit unknowingly, to validate that Evan was, indeed, an exemplary candidate for the leadership position. This is the power of your initial imprint, and it impacts your professional identity. It's the ambition of every leader in service and duty to be seen instantly as competent and capable, maximizing every opportunity to exhibit their leadership potential in public service and operational impact.

Your professional identity is a narrative, a story told from multiple perspectives—one you tell yourself, one that others tell to your face but, most important, one they tell behind your back.

Like every story, your professional identity narrative has a starting point. Think of it as the cover of a book that intrigues you. Once you've decided to buy into the cover and purchase the book you keep reading, page by page, further reinforcing whether your decision was worth it. It might be so boring that you give up after the first chapters, or it might be so exciting you can't wait to finish it and, even better, you hope there will be another book in the series.

Similarly, your professional identity starts with the initial impression—the cover. If this cover is compelling people will delve deeper, seeking to understand the full narrative of your leadership. If the story is compelling, people will want to keep reading. They will look forward to every new chapter, reinforcing their positive perceptions and anticipating more from you. In contrast, if the initial pages are disappointing, they might not continue reading, and your opportunity to influence and lead may be lost.

Your professional identity helps you create a story that others want to be a part of, a narrative they trust and believe. Just like an intriguing book cover and a captivating story, your professional identity should draw people in, keep them engaged, and leave them eagerly anticipating the next chapter in your leadership journey.

And, once again, we need to realize that a book is often purchased based on its visual appeal. Surely the title matters, maybe the author's name as well, and a recommendation can sway our choice, but even then, when we find ourselves scrolling through

online bookstores, the books with the striking covers are the ones that instantly stand out or reinforce what the title, author, and recommendation promise.

These critical moments of visual assessment can happen in any public service environment. Instead of the interview situation noted above, Matt could have been an analyst discussing strategy improvements in a regional planning session, or Evan could have been an advocate presenting a proposal for expanded community programs. Or Matt could have been a field officer conducting site visits for a public project, while Evan might have been leading a panel discussion on innovative ways to engage constituents in local governance.

The context may vary, but the specific situation matters less than the universal truth: Within those first crucial moments, based on their self-presentation, people are categorized as either "doubtful" or "promising" in their ability to lead.

And wouldn't you rather be the one with the exceptional book cover for your leadership narrative, the one that instantly stands out without having to say a word? Wouldn't you want to be one with a cover that catches the eye, intrigues the mind, and leaves a lasting impression, even before the first page is turned? Wouldn't you want to be the one that clearly invested in a professional book designer rather than just downloading an average template?

Just as a book cover can captivate a potential reader, your professional identity should captivate those around you. This is not about superficiality; it's about presenting the best version of yourself as a leader in service and duty. Your visual presentation serves as the cover of your professional identity. It's what draws others in and encourages them to look deeper, to turn the pages, and to invest in the narrative you want to tell about your approach to leadership.

So why settle for anything less than an extraordinary cover? Why not invest in every detail of your presentation, ensuring it aligns with the values and strengths you wish to project as a leader in service and duty?

And think about what impact this intentional choice could have on you. For starters, you wouldn't be a forgotten, dust-covered book left behind on a shelf or an overlooked title in an online listing. But you've already picked up this book, indicating that you recognize the importance of this topic for yourself as a professional dedicated to service and duty, and here you are, still engaged and turning pages.

So it will come as no surprise that your look of leadership shapes not only how you're perceived by others but also how you perceive yourself. Looking the part can significantly enhance your confidence and effectiveness as a leader in service and duty. The visual choices we make can act as a form of self-expression, offering a visual language that communicates our identity, mood, and confidence level—not just to others but also to ourselves. When a leader in service and duty wears clothes that align with their role and that they feel good in, it can create a positive feedback loop: They may feel more assertive, confident, and in control, which can, in turn, elevate their performance and the quality of their interactions with their teams and the communities they serve.

For many leaders in service and duty the right outfit serves as armor against the world, providing a sense of preparedness for whatever the day may bring, whether it's a contentious public meeting or a critical briefing to government officials. There's a reason terms like "power dressing" have emerged; clothing can be empowering, especially in a field where leaders are constantly under scrutiny from their teams and the public.

Research by Hajo Adam and Adam D. Galinsky from Northwestern University has shown that, when you dress in a way that you perceive as powerful, you can experience psychological changes that include increased abstract thinking, a key component of leadership. This intersection of clothing and psychology is known as "enclothed cognition," which describes the impact clothes have on the wearer's psychological processes. Enclothed cognition is a powerful testament to how the external—the professional identity we present—intersects with the internal, shaping how we perceive ourselves and, in turn, how we're perceived.

But is it really just about our clothing? Is our visual presence the sole driver of either our self-perception or how others perceive us? Clearly, it is not, yet it is significant. Our visual presence acts as a critical filter through which our professional behaviors and communications are perceived. It's a silent but powerful language that precedes and punctuates every action, whether we're presenting a budget proposal, meeting with agency directors, or representing our department at a public event.

There's a famous study by Albert Mehrabian that suggests the words you say—the actual words, not the tone or inflection—account for only 7 percent of the imprint you make. It's called the 7 percent-38 percent-55 percent rule. Words account for 7 percent, tone of voice accounts for 38 percent, and body language accounts for 55 percent of the imprint you make. We might think (or might have heard) that this study suggests it's not important what you say or how you behave; it's only about appearance. Of course, that's not true. That's another internet myth, and Mehrabian himself made countless attempts to clarify that the study should not be interpreted in such a way.

Still, countless coaches, trainers, and speakers use his study to suggest the thing that matters most is how you appear, neglecting the significance of verbal communication and behavior.

But if you have only a few seconds to make a first impression, your visual presence does take on greater importance. As I've noted, no one is exempt from this instinctive process; it's a fundamental aspect of our human cognition.

You'll recall that Matt and Evan had virtually identical résumés. (This is not just a hypothetical; in today's competitive public service landscape, among dozens of qualified applicants for a given position, there are bound to be several candidates who look virtually the same on paper.) The chances are that, when Christine first met Evan and Matt and they had a conversation—that is, during the first few seconds—there wasn't much difference in the actual words the two men spoke.

Those initial moments are too fleeting to demonstrate your competence in leadership. Instead, in such brief encounters it's our visual and our sensed presence that speaks volumes. Remember, in its quest for instant understanding, the human brain relies primarily on the visual cues it receives, complemented by the subtle undercurrents of what it feels rather than what it hears.

As Matt and Evan awaited their turns in the lobby, silent narratives unfolded within moments of Christine's approach. Those silent narratives cast a long and, sometimes, indelible shadow, setting a stage where unseen forces come into play. Those forces, subtle yet powerful, influenced the trajectory of Christine's judgments. Like invisible threads, they pulled at the fabric of perception, weaving assumptions and conclusions based on the initial visual encounter. Those forces elevated Evan in a halo of positive light, but they shrouded Matt in a cloud of skepticism.

When I speak at conferences, I usually demonstrate this issue by entering the stage and saying nothing. A long, uncomfortable silence envelops the room, one I create purposefully to ensure my audience members scrutinize only my visual presence.

Then I start counting out loud to seven, demonstrating just how fleeting this time frame is. This is the first time the audience hears my voice, registers my accent, and gauges my tone. It's the opening page in the narrative I'll write on stage, following the cover they've already judged. I confront them with a plethora of decisions they have already made about me without knowing anything about my background, skills, knowledge, or the value I bring to the event. And it's highly likely that dozens of audience members will approach me afterward and say something along the lines, "How did you know? What magic or witchcraft did you apply to read our minds?"

The reality is much simpler. It's a combination of the wardrobe choice I intentionally made, the audience I investigated, and the insights from years of my own research as well as that of Dr. Solomon and others. And even if the way this research has been described on the internet cannot be taken at face value, what it clarifies is which elements and thoughts of the eleven factors

become more relevant, depending on the situation you're in. For example, in an interview situation such as the one Matt and Evan experienced with Christine, critical attributes like competence, honesty, credibility, and trustworthiness are paramount in assessing a candidate's potential.

Imagine you're in a community meeting. Here, different elements come into play. Your level of empathy and commitment to community needs may be under a brighter spotlight as constituents gauge your suitability based on different criteria than in a traditional professional setting. And it's likely that your ability to listen and communicate effectively takes on greater relevance. Although the eleven elements remain consistent, their weightings shift based on the observer's motives.

So how can you reinforce the crucial elements? How can you better highlight and ensure the focus remains on what matters? By using the tools you already have. No, this book isn't about discovering some hidden secret or acquiring new tools. You already possess everything you need in your repertoire; it's simply a matter of applying those tools more intentionally in your leadership role.

The ABCDEs of Your Professional Identity

Your professional identity encompasses the multifaceted blend of choices you make—small or large—that shape how you're perceived and valued in your role as a leader. And this professional identity is the total of your choices in the following five areas:

- Appearance
- Behavior
- Communication
- Digital footprint
- Environment

Here's an easy way to remember these five key elements: ABCDE.

APPEARANCE: Your appearance is your first opportunity to make a statement without saying a word. It's the canvas upon which your personality is painted; it's how the initial impression you leave on your team and the public is formed. From the moment someone lays eyes on you, they're subconsciously processing a wealth of information about who you are and what you represent as a leader in service and duty.

In your sector, authority and trust play a particularly crucial role, and much of it is conveyed through visual elements. This is most evident in the symbolic power of uniforms, which are a cornerstone of many roles in public service. The sight of a uniform instantly communicates legitimacy, order, and purpose, reflecting the values and mission of the agencies they represent.

But even for those who don't regularly wear uniforms, visual presentation still carries significant weight. As leaders in the public eye, they are often perceived as representatives of official opinions, results, or decisions. Their appearance becomes a symbol of professionalism and accountability. Given the increased frequency of their public interactions compared to many other industries, their visual identity plays an outsized role in shaping perceptions.

Hence, clothing is your armor in the battlefield of first impressions. The fit, brand, style, quality, patterns, and colors of your clothes silently communicate your taste, personality, and attention to detail. Whether it's a tailored suit for a high-level meeting, a neatly pressed uniform for fieldwork, or polished business casual attire for community outreach, your appearance must consistently align with the authority, trust, and reliability your role demands.

Your personal grooming is the final touch that completes your appearance. Skin care, hair care, dental hygiene, and nail maintenance all contribute to your overall presentation. In your sector, the absence of meticulous grooming can inadvertently signal a lack of discipline or preparedness, traits that are especially scrutinized by the public.

Your appearance is a silent language that speaks volumes about who you are and how you approach life—and your career.

It allows you to set the stage for meaningful connections and interactions with your team and the public. It's not just about looking good; it's about embodying the values and confidence you want to project. When you appear with intention, you send a powerful message to the world that you're ready to lead, succeed, and make an impact in service and duty.

BEHAVIOR: At the core of your behavior lies your attitude, the vibrant colors that illuminate your outlook, ranging from sunny optimism to somber clouds of negativity. Your attitude not only sets the tone for your interactions but also serves as a compass to guide you through your career in public service.

Adding depth to your behavior is your charisma (or lack thereof), drawing others into your orbit with your irresistible charm, that magnetic force that most of us wish to have.

Navigating this rich tapestry of behavior requires emotional intelligence, the wisdom to read between the lines and steer gracefully through the intricate labyrinth of human interaction. For leaders in this sector, emotional intelligence is particularly critical, as such leaders often manage diverse teams, address sensitive issues with constituents, and negotiate complex political and social dynamics.

But no masterpiece is complete without a sturdy foundation of ethics and morals, the bedrock upon which your character as a leader in service and duty stands firm. In fact, integrity and moral consistency are nonnegotiable in your sector where the public's trust is both the currency and the measure of success. Every decision and action you take is viewed as a reflection of the values you uphold, and any perceived lapse in integrity can have far-reaching consequences, not just for your career but for the trust placed in your agency as a whole.

As you navigate the vast canvas of human interaction, diplomacy and courtesy should be your guiding stars. Your behavior is the brushstroke that adds depth and dimension to your professional identity.

It's the unwavering commitment to integrity, empathy, and respect that sets you apart. In every interaction, let your conduct reflect the leader you aspire to be, because only through consistent, intentional behavior can you build a legacy of trust and influence.

COMMUNICATION: The most important part of communication doesn't involve words. Instead, at the heart of communication lies active listening, the art of tuning in to others. Through active listening you not only hear the words spoken by team members and constituents, you also understand the emotions and intentions behind them. Adding depth to your communication are your body language and facial expressions, the nonverbal and silent-yet-eloquent language of gestures, postures, and movements. Your body and face speak volumes, conveying emotions and attitudes that words alone cannot express.

And what melody is complete without your voice, the instrument you play every single day. Your voice, with its range of tones, pitches, and cadences, is vital to delivering your message. From the gentle lilt of persuasion when engaging with community members to the commanding resonance of authority when leading a team briefing, each vocal element adds depth and richness to your communication.

Words themselves are the very essence of communication, and your language palette is the paintbrush with which you craft your message. Yet it's not just what you say but how you say it that shapes the narrative of your communication. Your communication habits, whether empathetic and concise or passive and manipulative, set the tone for your interactions, guiding the flow of every conversation and shaping the dynamics of relationships. Your accent or dialect may add richness and diversity to these conversations.

For leaders in service and duty, communication carries a unique weight. Unlike in other sectors where messages may primarily circulate within internal teams, leaders in service and duty often find their words scrutinized by the public.

This fact amplifies the challenge of communication, as even well-intentioned statements can be misinterpreted or taken out of context. Balancing clarity, precision, and empathy becomes critical to ensuring that the intended message resonates accurately and avoids misunderstandings that could undermine trust.

Your written communication is the ink that flows through the veins of our interconnected world, from memos to team members to statements addressing the public. In your sector, written communication often involves additional scrutiny or compliance with regulations, further underscoring the need for precision and care.

Effective communication bridges gaps, builds trust, and fosters collaboration. Every conversation is an opportunity to reinforce your professional identity, so speak with clarity, listen with empathy, and engage with purpose.

DIGITAL FOOTPRINT: Your digital footprint is like a breadcrumb trail scattered across the internet with each crumb leaving its mark on your online reputation. From intentional actions to those unwittingly left behind, each interaction shapes not only your digital presence in the first step but also your offline persona.

At the heart of this trail lies email communication, a digital handshake that speaks volumes about your professionalism and reliability. Similarly, your mobile communication offers glimpses into your accessibility and efficiency as a leader.

Venturing into social media, your posts, comments, likes, and shares, can enhance your online reputation, positioning you as a credible and insightful voice within your digital community.

In your sector, certain roles may come with restrictions on social media use or expectations for neutrality in public-facing communications. Email communication, too, may be subject to regulations governing record-keeping, confidentiality, or public access to information that necessitates a heightened level of diligence and professionalism. Leaders must navigate these constraints while maintaining a credible and approachable digital presence.

In virtual meetings with team members or community leaders, your digital footprint takes on a new dimension, showcasing your adaptability and professionalism in remote settings.

Meanwhile, chats and forums serve as arenas for digital discourse where your contributions reflect your expertise, engagement, credibility, and influence within online communities.

The frequency, savviness, and authenticity of your digital interactions shape your unintentional footprint, influencing how you're perceived in the digital realm.

Your digital footprint is the modern extension of your professional identity. In an age when digital presence is pivotal, your digital actions and interactions can amplify your credibility or undermine it. Be mindful of the digital legacy you create. Every post, comment, and message contributes to the narrative of who you are. Curate your digital footprint with the same care and intention as your physical presence.

ENVIRONMENT: Your environment isn't just where you are, it's the vibrant backdrop against which your professional journey in public service unfolds, filled with both tangible and intangible elements that shape your daily experiences and leave an indelible mark.

In your sector, your environment is under constant observation. Even as leaders strive to maintain neutrality, the public often subconsciously interprets details about their surroundings—whether it's who they associate with or the choices they make in their workspace—as indicative of their leanings or priorities. This creates an added layer of pressure, as every aspect of their environment can inadvertently influence perceptions.

Moreover, since many roles in this sector are funded by public resources, often there is a heightened level of scrutiny about how those resources are allocated and used. From office furnishings to travel expenses, every detail may be viewed through the lens of public accountability, requiring leaders to balance functionality and transparency in their choices.

Your network, for example, isn't just a list of contacts; it's a living ecosystem that provides support, fosters collaboration, and unlocks doors of opportunity at every turn.

Then there are the spaces you inhabit, the places you live, work, and everything in between. Those spaces are more than just physical locations; they're sanctuaries of productivity, creativity, and inspiration. This could be your office in a government building, the community centers you visit, or the remote field locations you oversee.

And let's not forget about the journey itself, the daily commute, the occasional getaway, and the leisure pursuits that recharge your batteries. From the thrill of exploring new destinations to the tranquility of downtime, these experiences add color to the canvas of your professional life, infusing it with excitement, balance, and rejuvenation.

Your environment isn't just a backdrop; it's a character in the story of your professional journey in public service, shaping the plot and influencing the outcomes at every twist and turn. So take a moment to look around. What do you see? How does it make you feel? And, most important, how can you optimize it to support your goals, reflect your values, and lead you toward success and fulfillment?

Your professional identity is a mosaic of countless pieces, each carefully chosen and placed to create a masterpiece that is uniquely you. From your appearance to your behavior, your communication, your digital footprint, and your environment—every element—plays a vital role in shaping how you're perceived and valued as a leader. Each piece of this mosaic works together to create a comprehensive and compelling professional identity.

Yes, and although an impeccable look can open doors, it's your behavior and communication that will sustain those connections. Simply looking great is insufficient; your actions and words must consistently support the professional identity created by your appearance.

In your sector, this interplay becomes even more crucial, as leaders are not only judged by their visual presentation but also by their perceived authority, ethics, and ability to represent public trust effectively. As noted, authority is often visually expressed through uniforms, powerful symbols of responsibility and credibility. Even for those who don't wear uniforms, their visual presence remains a potent signal to a public that frequently evaluate them as representatives of official decisions. But if your actions or communication falter, any positive impressions created by appearance can quickly erode, emphasizing the importance of consistency and integrity across all facets of leadership.

In today's digital age, your digital footprint holds immense relevance, often serving as the first impression team members or constituents encounter, or it can reshape opinions after in-person interactions. For instance, a public official championing a community initiative might be evaluated online by potential supporters before they decide to back the effort. Alternatively, a leader in a regulatory role might leave a positive impression initially, but subsequent scrutiny of their digital footprint—such as social media activity or inconsistent statements—can reshape opinions. These examples demonstrate how digital presence continues to influence perceptions, both before and after pivotal moments. And additional complexities arise from regulatory constraints or the expectation of impartiality, making it essential to navigate online platforms with care.

Lastly, the environment you cultivate is a critical yet often underestimated aspect of your professional identity. For leaders in service and duty, environment includes both the physical spaces they occupy and the people they surround themselves with. The public—consciously or subconsciously—often assesses these environments as reflective of priorities or affiliations. Even non-partisan roles are subject to assumptions, as individuals infer leanings or biases from perceived associations. Creating an environment that supports your goals, reflects your values, and encourages growth is essential for sustaining a strong professional identity.

Only if each piece of this mosaic works together and is consistent across all these elements will a collection of good impressions transform into a lasting narrative. In the end, it's not just about making a strong first impression; it's about living up to that impression, day in and day out, in every public interaction, decision, and initiative.

Internal and External Consistency

Consistency is the backbone of any credible professional identity. The key is to ensure your ABCDEs all sing the same tune. You can't present yourself as reliable and trustworthy in your appearance but then behave unpredictably or unprofessionally during interactions with the public or with colleagues. You can't curate a digital presence that conflicts with who you are in real life. Representing yourself as a steward of public service while creating environments or narratives that suggest self-interest or partiality sends mixed messages. Using a professional tone in verbal communication but allowing written communications to contain errors or lack clarity undermines your perceived competence as a leader. Only when all elements of your professional identity align harmoniously does the message of who you are and what you stand for become unmistakable, compelling, and memorable. This consistency must extend beyond personal presentation, reflecting a coherent professional identity both within your agency and in the broader public sphere.

- **Internal consistency** refers to how you present yourself, behave, and communicate within the intricate ecosystem of your agency. This encompasses your daily interactions with your team, cross-agency collaborations, or engagements with senior leaders. Leaders who demonstrate unwavering consistency in their professional identity within this internal sphere earn the respect and trust of their colleagues, fostering a culture of integrity and accountability.

Think about the ripple effect of your actions, how your steadfast commitment to transparency and excellence can inspire your team, strengthen collaboration across departments, and drive impactful outcomes for the group you serve. Reflect on how every decision, every interaction, and every message contributes to the larger narrative of your leadership within public service.

- **External consistency**, on the other hand, pertains to how you represent yourself and your agency to the public. Every interaction—whether it's a community town hall, a press conference, a speaking engagement, or even a casual conversation with a local resident—showcases your professional identity. The impressions you create in these moments extend far beyond your personal reputation; they influence how your agency and its mission are perceived within the public eye. Imagine the weight of responsibility you carry as a leader whose words and actions can bolster trust in agencies or, conversely, sow seeds of doubt. Your professional presence is a living testament to your dedication to impartiality, ethics, and the broader objectives of public service.

But this principle, while seemingly straightforward, encompasses a complex and nuanced challenge that extends beyond individual effort. The true test of a leader lies in ensuring this consistency permeates the entire team. Your challenge isn't just about maintaining your own standards, it's also about inspiring and fostering adherence to these standards across all team members. When the entire team upholds shared values and norms, it creates unity and professionalism, reinforcing public trust and confidence in the agency. Conversely, inconsistencies among team members can introduce doubt that undermines the agency's credibility and, by extension, your professional identity as its leader.

It's vital for your team to understand that their appearance, behavior, communication, digital presence, and environment—both inside and outside the agency—reflect on you and the mission you represent. While many team members diligently adhere to internal protocols in the workplace, it's easy to inadvertently overlook these standards in personal or informal settings.

Picture this: You're addressing a legislative committee or hosting a community outreach event, representing your agency's goals and accomplishments. You've meticulously prepared, honing your presentation to reflect the professionalism and ethical standards you champion. In that moment, every detail of your appearance, your demeanor, and your tone underscores your agency's commitment to public service. Now imagine that, elsewhere in the room, a member of your team is present but unaware of how their actions might be perceived. Perhaps they're dressed in a way that contradicts the formality of the occasion. Or maybe they're engaged in unprofessional behavior, like speaking out of turn or failing to show respect for other attendees. In this scenario, the contrast between your professional presence and the actions of your team member creates a discord that undermines the cohesive image you've worked so hard to build. Even if your performance is exemplary, the behavior of a single team member can cast a shadow on your leadership and the agency's reputation.

Or consider this: A team member who consistently demonstrates impeccable professionalism in face-to-face meetings suddenly posts personal or controversial opinions online that conflict with the agency's values or mission. While the posts may reflect their personal views, they also create an inconsistency that could lead to questions about the agency's culture or oversight. The public doesn't always distinguish between personal and professional boundaries when evaluating public servants, making it even more crucial to manage these perceptions.

When everyone is aligned and presenting a united front, it strengthens the collective credibility of the agency. Conversely, inconsistencies—intentional or inadvertent—can lead to public confusion and erode trust in your team's ability to serve effectively.

Maintaining this internal and external consistency is not solely the responsibility of leaders; it's a shared responsibility that extends to every team member. If this resonates with you as a familiar challenge, you'll be pleased to know that another chapter of this book will delve deeper into techniques for effectively addressing these challenges with your team, providing tips and insights to support you in having these sensitive conversations.

Nowadays, where scrutiny is constant and public opinion is swift, you and your team are always in the spotlight. There's little room to hide. Every action, interaction, and communication can be observed, dissected, and evaluated. Your professional identity thrives on visibility, but it's not just about being seen; it's about ensuring what's seen aligns with the values you stand for. Your leadership isn't just about crafting a professional identity, it's about making sure it's consistent, credible, and resonates across all platforms, both in-person and online. By ensuring consistency in your team's actions and attitudes, you amplify your own leadership visibility, cultivating a unified and compelling identity that earns respect and trust from all who observe it.

From Shadows to Spotlight

A picture-perfect professional identity that remains hidden in the shadows serves no one. Hence, in one of my other books, *Discover Your Fair Advantage*, I dive extensively into the different visibility levels that exist in any work environment. If you haven't picked up a copy of that book yet, I invite you to do so. Your professional library will thank you, and so will your career, because the book is like a professional supercharge. But for now, let's revisit these visibility levels and explore what they mean for your professional identity. As we journey through these levels, you might find yourself recognizing where you currently stand and where you aspire to be.

Visibility level 1—being invisible: Some leaders in service and duty operate under the radar, their efforts unnoticed, despite their significance. They might blend into the background, performing critical tasks without recognition from senior leaders. These leaders remain largely unknown, their contributions hidden behind a veil of anonymity. This invisibility can stem from a lack of confidence, insufficient skills to stand out, or inexperience in navigating the competitive landscape of their agency. Some may even choose this path consciously, seeking to avoid unwanted attention or additional responsibilities. But for others, this invisibility is not a choice but a circumstance they struggle to change. Their potential remains untapped, waiting for an opportunity that might never come. This level makes senior leaders ask, "Who is this person, and what do they do in our agency?" At this level, your professional identity is faint, almost indistinguishable, and it lacks the clarity needed to be recognized and valued. Your appearance seems nondescript, blending in with the crowd. Your behavior might come across as passive, failing to draw attention. Your communication may be limited or unnoticed. Your digital footprint may be minimal, and your environment unremarkable.

Visibility level 2—being common: Achieving a basic level of visibility as a leader in service and duty means being recognized for your consistent performance. You're known for doing a good job, but there's nothing that sets you apart. You become a reliable yet common presence in the workplace, acknowledged for your contributions but not seen as a unique asset. Senior leaders may recognize your name and associate you with a role, yet they may not perceive you as someone who can add exceptional value in new or challenging roles. You're seen as dependable but interchangeable. This common visibility makes senior leaders think, *They do a pretty good job managing their team or overseeing this initiative, but what else?* At this level, your professional identity is stable yet unremarkable, blending into the background. Your behavior might be seen as competent but routine, without showcasing unique qualities. Your communication may be clear and functional but not particularly memorable or influential. Your digital footprint may be consistent but unremarkable, reflecting a standard presence without distinction, and your environment might be generic.

Visibility level 3—being unique: At this level you have moved beyond mere competence as a leader in service and duty and have started to demonstrate unique capabilities and assets. You stand out among your colleagues and are recognized for specific strengths that add unique value to your role and agency. This visibility is not easily achieved; it requires self-awareness, confidence, and dedication to highlight what makes you unique. You are known for doing exceptional work in a way that's distinctively yours, whether it's implementing innovative community programs, pioneering sustainable practices in public infrastructure, or developing unique solutions for complex challenges. Senior leadership begins to identify you as a valuable resource, considering you for opportunities that require the specific attributes you consistently showcase. This visibility level prompts senior leaders to say, "This leader is an outstanding performer with a unique approach that benefits our agency." At this level your professional identity is clear, distinctive, and marked by specific strengths that set you apart. Your appearance may be distinguished by unique elements that reflect your professional identity. Your behavior might be characterized by a proactive approach that sets you apart. Your communication may be impactful and memorable, clearly conveying your unique perspective and value. Your digital footprint may be strategic and engaging, showcasing your expertise and thought leadership in public service. Your environment might be thoughtfully curated to reflect your standards of excellence.

Visibility level 4—being referrable: At the highest level of visibility, your unique strengths and capabilities are not only recognized but also advocated by others. You're referred and recommended for opportunities without your direct involvement. Your reputation precedes you, and senior leaders discuss your

potential in high-level meetings, often considering you for promotions or new roles because of your well-known and unique assets. This level of visibility ensures you're seen as an irreplaceable asset to the agency, and it significantly enhances your career trajectory. Senior leadership is likely to say, "Have you heard about this leader? They're incredible at community engagement or driving policy innovation or managing high-profile initiatives and perfect for this new opportunity." At this level your professional identity is robust, influential, and continuously promoted by others, making you a sought-after leader within and outside your agency. Your appearance may exude a commanding presence that is instantly recognizable and respected. Your behavior might be seen as exemplary, consistently demonstrating leadership qualities that inspire and motivate others. Your communication may be highly influential with your words carrying significant weight in discussions. Your digital footprint may be extensive and authoritative, positioning you as a go-to expert in your field. Your environment might be a reflection of your high standards and success, reinforcing your professional identity through its exceptional quality and attention to detail.

Did you find yourself in one of these levels? Ultimately, visibility level 1 (being invisible) will prove to be detrimental to your leadership career. Even visibility level 2 (being common) prevents you from being noticed. When your visibility stagnates at those levels, you might often think, *Everybody knows I'm doing good work in this department, so why am I not getting ahead?*

And I know how that feels. I was stuck in visibility level 2 for many years during my corporate career. I was a hard worker, deeply committed to the success of my organization and its senior leaders, and I received plenty of recognition from my leaders for my outstanding results and work ethic. They knew they could count on me for any task, and I was involved in a variety of projects. Yet, when opportunities arose, my name was never mentioned, even though I knew exactly what I was capable of offering and had the necessary assets.

Now I understand that it isn't enough to simply be known for being good at something. There are many leaders out there just like you and me—hardworking and reliable. In my journey from visibility level 2 to higher levels I had to intentionally work on every aspect of my professional identity. My transformation began with a deliberate focus on my appearance. I reevaluated my wardrobe choices and my look to ensure it reflected the leadership status I wanted to project. I turned my attention to my behavior and forced myself to become more proactive in meetings, sharing my insights confidently and ensuring my contributions were noticed. I refined my communication skills, both spoken and written, ensuring I was clear, concise, and impactful. I strategically curated my digital presence, ensuring my social media profiles and professional networks reflected my expertise and achievements. This effort involved proactively creating content that showcased my knowledge and engaged others in my field. I also paid closer attention to my environment. I surrounded myself with individuals who supported my growth and challenged me to excel, which meant I had to let go of many other people. Through these intentional efforts I transformed my professional identity from common to unique, from overlooked to referrable. That holistic approach ensured every facet of my professional identity worked in harmony, allowing me to stand out.

The key to reaching visibility level 3 (being unique) or 4 (being referrable) is to stand out from the crowd and to be instantly and consistently visible to senior leaders within your agency and sector. Only such visibility will bring attention to what you do, how you do it and, most important, who is doing it—*you*.

Your goal is not just to craft an exceptional professional identity; you need to ensure it's recognized and remembered. The more refined and intentional this identity is, the easier it is to achieve those objectives. This effort requires relentless self-awareness, strategic visibility, and a steadfast foundation of confidence in yourself as a leader.

Chapter 3
Leaders Look Confident

Confidence Isn't Thinking You're Better. It's Realizing You Have No Reason to Compare Yourself.

Chapter 3: Leaders Look Confident

Think of a skyscraper, a marvel of modern engineering, reaching toward the sky with its gleaming windows and impressive facade. What keeps this towering structure standing strong, day after day, year after year? It's the foundation—the unseen, unsung hero that lies beneath the surface that provides the stability and strength that allows the building to rise above the rest. Sure, the design, materials, and craftsmanship all play crucial roles, but it all starts with a solid foundation. Without it, even the most impressive architectural feats would be destined to crumble. Like a skyscraper, a leader in service and duty's success is built upon a foundation—not one of concrete and steel but of confidence. It's the bedrock upon which a leaders' professional identity is constructed, the invisible architecture that supports their every move in the multifaceted and high-pressure world of public service.

But what, exactly, is confidence? What does it mean to look confident, and why would it even matter for a leader? First, confidence isn't just about having a firm belief in your own abilities or the decisions you make. It's much more than that. It's also about having an aura of competence, empathy, and unwavering authority that inspires trust, respect, and a sense of security in everyone around you, whether it's senior leaders, team members, constituents, or the broader public. Few qualities are more essential than an unwavering sense of confidence. This inner belief in your abilities to adapt, persist, and succeed is a prerequisite for thriving amid the constant rejections, scrutiny, and uncertainties inherent in public service.

Research has repeatedly explored this vital link between confidence and leadership performance. Studies by Robert S. Heiser at the University of Maine and David McArthur at Utah Valley University affirm confidence and enthusiasm have long been recognized as prerequisites for exceptional leadership. Their findings suggest the most successful leaders exude an air of confidence that allows them to remain adaptive and resilient in their approaches. Similarly, a research paper by Guangping Wang at Louisiana State University indicates leaders with higher levels of confidence tend to outperform their less confident counterparts. An inner reserve of belief empowers them to invest greater effort, even when facing repeated setbacks and naysayers.

But confidence, the foundation of your professional identity, often finds itself besieged by a multitude of enemies. These adversaries lurk in the shadows and can chip away at the confidence of even the most self-assured leader in service and duty. Let's explore some of these saboteurs and how they might impact you.

Comparison—the thief of joy and confidence: It's so easy and common to fall into a cycle of continuously comparing yourself to others. You might find yourself measuring your performance, achievements, and even your own worth against others. It's a subtle process that can chip away at your confidence and leave you feeling inadequate. Imagine this: You've made significant strides in your department, but you can't help comparing your outcomes to another leader's highly publicized successes. Every time you weigh your accomplishments against theirs, it's like a small piece of your confidence erodes. It's a common tendency, but it's crucial to recognize that comparison is the thief of joy and confidence. True confidence comes from within.

Rejection—the constant companion of leadership: Rejection is an ever-present challenge in public service, like the uninvited guest to the leadership party. As a leader you might face countless rejections, such as a declined proposal for a community initiative, unanswered outreach from a key stakeholder, or even

public pushback on a policy you championed. Each rejection can feel like a personal setback, gradually eroding your confidence. But rejection is part of the territory in public service. Confidence requires turning those rejections into opportunities for growth. It's about understanding that every rejection brings you one step closer to an acceptance. Most important, it's about having the resilience to keep pushing forward, no matter how many obstacles you face.

Imposter syndrome—the inner critic: Do you sometimes hear that nagging voice in your head that whispers, "You're a fraud," even when you're succeeding in your role? The higher you climb up the leadership ladder, the louder that voice can become. You might start questioning whether you deserve your role, especially when working in a public sector that demands constant scrutiny and accountability. Perhaps you wonder if your decisions are good enough for public trust or if your success is merely luck. Imposter syndrome can be particularly challenging to overcome in fields where scrutiny is high and metrics of success are not always tangible. The key is to own your achievements, reminding yourself that your success is the result of your hard work, talent, and determination. You belong exactly where you are.

Public accountability and pressure—the weight of expectation: The pressure to meet and exceed expectations can be relentless. You're constantly under scrutiny with your decisions, public statements, and outcomes all being closely monitored. You may feel the weight of public opinion, knowing a single misstep could lead to mistrust. When a community initiative doesn't meet its goals or a budget is scrutinized by taxpayers, it's easy to start doubting yourself. But true confidence comes from focusing on the process, not just the result. It's about trusting in your ability to adapt, innovate, and lead your team through challenging times. It's about maintaining a steadfast belief in yourself and your team, even when faced with setbacks.

The rapid pace of change—staying ahead of the curve: The public service landscape is constantly evolving. New regulations, shifting public expectations, and technological advancements can make it challenging to stay confident in the face of rapid change. You might worry about keeping up with legal changes, evolving societal needs, or implementing new technologies effectively. But confidence is about embracing change. It's about committing to continuous learning, being willing to experiment and adapt, and believing in your ability to navigate uncharted territory. It's about leaning into the discomfort of the unknown and trusting in your resilience and adaptability as a leader.

Confidence is a complex concept built from a combination of internal and external factors. While the psychological battle against these enemies is ongoing, there is one powerful weapon in a leader's arsenal that can help shield against these confidence saboteurs: your visual presence. At first glance the link between your look of leadership and confidence might seem superficial, like it's just about "dressing the part." But the impact of your external presentation on your internal confidence is far more significant than you might think. With all the challenges and self-doubts that leaders face, a powerful look of leadership can serve as a suit of armor, a tangible reminder—for yourself and others—of your professionalism, competence, and readiness to lead. So let's explore the internal dimension of dressing with confidence.

Dress for the confidence you want, not the insecurities you have. It's a universally acknowledged truth that when we look good, we feel good. This isn't shallow vanity. It's a reflection of how closely intertwined our self-esteem and self-perception are with our external appearance. Clothes do more than just cover us up; they can make us feel good or uneasy, especially at work. In their article "Dress, Body and Self: Research on the Social Psychology of Dress," researcher Kim K. P. Johnson and her team found that when professionals dressed appropriately for their job, they felt more confident. The team's research revealed that professionals

associated psychological discomfort with wearing inappropriate dress for work. Mary Katherine Brock confirmed that young professionals' confidence is heavily influenced by the clothes they wear. Even color seems to matter, as Craig Roberts and his research team pointed out, because certain colors, such as red, can boost individual confidence. Or you might remember the research I mentioned by Hajo Adam and Adam D. Galinsky who introduced the concept of enclothed cognition, which means what we wear can change the way we think and feel. Their study focused on the significance of wearing white coats in the medical field and how such attire impacts mental processes. The researchers discovered that wearing a white coat can sharpen a person's focus and attention to detail. But the effect varied based on the described purpose of the coat: white coats belonging to doctors enhanced attentiveness more so than painters' coats did. This finding indicates the influence of clothing on cognitive function depends on both symbolic association and the physical act of wearing the garment.

The leader's armor of a well-considered wardrobe serves not just as a physical outfit but also as a psychological booster. What we decide to wear every day can shape how we feel about ourselves and how we interact. How often have you felt a dip in confidence because of a poorly chosen outfit for a crucial meeting with a stakeholder or public official? Have you ever cringed when a constituent mentioned they found your social media profile, knowing you have an outdated picture that doesn't reflect your current role? Have you ever walked into an important meeting only to realize your shirt has an obvious stain? Have you noticed how a cluttered background visible on a video call detracted from the professional identity you aimed to project?

By taking the time to create a look of leadership that exudes capability, authority, and self-assurance, you're not just influencing how others see you, you're engaging in a powerful act of self-affirmation. You're telling yourself that you're worthy of investment, that you're prepared to face the challenges of the day, and that you're capable of handling whatever comes your way, from addressing public concerns to implementing policy decisions.

Dress with intention and style and then inspire with substance. Leaders who exude confidence through their visual presence subconsciously garner more attention than those who do not. A confident leader's presence instantly captivates, signaling expertise worth listening to. You've likely experienced leaders who walk into a room—perhaps a town hall meeting, a public event, or a community forum—and fill it with an undeniable aura of authority and charisma. It's as if their very presence commands respect and admiration. They carry themselves with a certain poise, a self-assuredness that's unmistakable. Their posture is upright, their movements purposeful, and their gaze direct and engaging. It's not just about what they wear, but how they wear it.

When you encounter such leaders, you can't help but wonder, *Where does this magnetic presence come from? What's the secret behind their unwavering self-assurance?* And then, as if to answer your unspoken questions, the leader begins to speak. Their words are articulate, their insights about public policy or community needs profound, and their vision for their agency or department compelling. They have the substance to back up their style, proving their confidence is not a facade but a reflection of their true capabilities.

This is the power of a leader who understands the importance of both the visual and the substantive aspects of leadership. They know their appearance is the first point of contact, the initial impression that sets the tone for all subsequent interactions. But they also recognize that their appearance is just the beginning—it's their expertise in public service operations, their decision-making skills, and their ability to inspire and motivate that sets them apart. When you, as a leader, take pride in your visual presence and couple it with genuine substance, you create an empowering culture of achievement. Your team members look up to you not just because you look the part but also because you embody the values and the vision of your agency. You lead by example, demonstrating that success is not just about looking good but about being good—good at what you do, good to your team, and good for the agency or community you represent.

Dress to spread confidence like a wildfire. Confidence is contagious, especially when it emanates from someone in a leadership position. The confident aura you cultivate and the intentionality behind your refined visual presence radiates outward, affecting your entire team's psyche and performance. When you carry yourself with confidence, it instills in your team members a sense of pride in who they work for and who they represent. They might begin emulating the high standards you embody, feeling inspired to show up as their best selves. Your confidence becomes their confidence. This ripple effect can extend far beyond your immediate team. It can permeate the entire agency, shaping its culture and reputation. When you, as a leader, consistently demonstrate confidence through your visual presence, it sends a powerful message to your team and the public, communicating stability, competence, and a commitment to excellence that inspires trust and respect within the public sphere.

Conversely, any glimpses of insecurity or half-hearted efforts can breed uncertainty among all ranks. If you seem uninspired in your presence, it gives permission for your team to underperform and make excuses. As the adage goes, "They will never care how much you know until they know how much you care." The contagious effect of a leader's confidence is, perhaps, the most pivotal force for elevating everyone's performance. So as we explore the "look of leadership" in the pages to come, let's approach visual appearance not as a superficial consideration but as a potent tool in the confidence-building arsenal of leadership.

Leaders Are Confident about Their Body

Think about ants. Despite their miniature size, ants achieve extraordinary things. They forge complex tunnels, transport massive loads, and collaborate with remarkable efficiency. The incredible strength and resilience packed into such a small creature show us that size and weight do not determine capability or value. Instead, it's about leveraging what you have to its fullest potential.

So let's start our discussion about confidence by setting aside the looks you can buy and focus on your most important one—the one you were born with—your body. Recognizing your body as a fundamental aspect of your identity and a vessel through which you offer leadership is the first step toward deeper self-confidence. You need to acknowledge your unique body characteristics—your strengths and your limitations—and embrace them as integral parts of who you are as a leader in service and duty.

Because who hasn't, at least once, wrangled with thoughts like these: *I'll never be taken seriously as a public official because I'm too short. How can I represent a health department if I can't even manage my own weight? I'm too tall, and people find me intimidating when I walk into a town hall meeting. I look so underweight. I don't appear strong enough to handle the challenges of this job.* It's natural to question ourselves. But it will come as no surprise that these self-destructive thoughts can undermine your confidence as a leader. The truth is your physical attributes don't define your leadership potential. Instead, you should leverage what you have to its fullest extent, just like those tiny ants that achieve extraordinary feats despite their size. And although there are some tricks when it comes to dressing your body, you'll never be able to fully change the fundamentals: someone short will never be tall; someone overweight is unlikely to ever look skinny. This acceptance is not resignation but a celebration of diversity and your individuality. Nevertheless, let's explore how weight and height impact perceptions of leadership.

Confidence beyond the scale: Weight is often perceived as a reflection of personal discipline and lifestyle. In various professional spheres, particularly those with a focus on health, fitness, or overall well-being, weight can influence perceptions of credibility and authority. Consider, for example, leaders in public health, emergency services, or the military where professionals often serve as role models for discipline and healthful living. In these fields the expectation is that your visual presence aligns with professional advice.

Similarly, leadership roles that demand a high degree of discipline and self-control also might scrutinize physical fitness as a proxy for these traits. Think of roles in law enforcement or fire services. In uniformed roles such as the military, physical fitness is not just a personal consideration but often a professional requirement. Standards for weight, body composition, and endurance are tied directly to operational readiness and the ability to fulfill demanding responsibilities. Such expectations can create additional scrutiny for leaders in these fields, as their physical fitness is often viewed as a symbol of their discipline and capability. For public-facing leaders, such as elected officials or spokespeople, physical appearance is often under the microscope. Public scrutiny of body image—whether tied to health, vitality, or discipline—can influence trust and confidence among constituents. Leaders in the public eye are frequently judged on their appearance with a healthy body often interpreted as a reflection of their competence and energy. Media exposure compounds this pressure. A single unflattering photo can overshadow a leader's message or achievements, unfairly shifting public focus to their physical traits rather than their capabilities or contributions. In public office, a leader's fitness and health can subtly influence public trust, as physical appearance often becomes linked to perceptions of competence and vitality. The connotation is this: If they can't maintain high standards for themselves, how can they effectively lead initiatives that impact public welfare?

When we talk about weight insecurities, our minds may instantly zero in on the overweight, but that's only half the story. Bias related to weight manifests in two opposing but equally damaging stereotypes: those who are heavier may be perceived as lacking self-control, whereas those who are thinner may be perceived as being too delicate to manage the stress and responsibilities of leadership. Both of these stereotypes are unjust and overlook the individual's actual capabilities and contributions. But most studies related to weight and bias in the workplace focus predominantly on the overweight perspective, often neglecting the challenges faced by those who are underweight.

For example, Patricia V. Roehling and her team highlighted how obesity affects perceptions of promotability, demonstrating that obese candidates are often seen as less suitable for promotions compared to individuals with other physical conditions. This bias also extends to leadership perceptions where obese individuals are significantly underrepresented in top positions within Fortune 100 companies. And T. L. Brink, supported by Eden B. King, revealed obesity can significantly influence views of a person's leadership abilities. In addition, Joseph A. Bellizzi and Ronald W. Hasty discovered that leaders broadly view obese professionals as less suited for challenging, client-facing responsibilities that demand constant engagement and presence. The discriminatory effects were lessened for roles involving minimal face-to-face client interactions, such as telephone positions. Perhaps most disconcertingly, the research indicated obese professionals face harsher disciplinary actions from their leaders when accused of ethical breaches or other misconduct.

But despite the impact of weight on professional perceptions, as various studies demonstrate, the most crucial factor is your own relationship with your body weight, because it can significantly influence your confidence as a leader. This internal perception of self-worth and assurance should be strong enough to override external biases and determine how you are viewed. Hence, if you're seeking to align your weight with your health goals and professional identity, options include the following:

Carry your weight with poise and confidence, no matter the number on the scale. You are who you are in the body you have, and it's no one's business why you're in this body. It could be health issues, eating habits, lifestyle choices, or even genetics. But remember that the right fit of clothing can significantly affect both how you perceive your weight and how others perceive it. Ill-fitting clothes can add pounds or create an unflattering, distracting silhouette. Conversely, well-tailored clothes can enhance your look of leadership, contributing positively to your confidence and overall perception.

The key is a strategic selection of clothing that fits impeccably, thus avoiding adding unnecessary bulk or implying a lack of attention to detail, either of which can detract from your professional identity.

And ignore any outdated and oversimplified methods of categorizing body shapes. You're more than an "apple" or a "pear"—you're a leader, a professional, a force, and an individual whose worth is defined by accomplishments and abilities, not by the contours of a silhouette. Your shape doesn't confine your potential; it's your presence and your actions that carve out the real shape of your influence and impact. Categorizing you by body shape, although once popular, not only pigeonholes you but also often overlooks the nuances and individuality of each person's style. It disregards the fact that, whereas some individuals may wish to downplay their "pear" shape, others may want to embrace and accentuate it with pride. No one-size-fits-all concept can dictate whether you should highlight or downplay your shape. It's your body and your style, so it's your rules.

Opt to lose or gain weight with a focus on health rather than solely on aesthetics. Yes, let's rip off that Band-Aid. There's no middle ground, no easy getaway, no shortcut. If you believe your weight, whether too heavy or too light, impacts the way you perceive yourself or the way others perceive your professional identity, you might need to apply disciplined, consistent, and consequent measures.

Positive changes in weight can lead to a boost in confidence and enhance your overall perception. Yet, as you probably know, this process should be undertaken with health as the priority, ensuring the journey toward weight change is sustainable and reflects a genuine commitment to your personal well-being. It's not just about the number on the scale but about nurturing a lifestyle that promotes your overall well-being. It's about recognizing that the objective isn't a specific aesthetic but a state of health where you feel most vibrant and capable.

Because here's the crux of the matter: it's no secret that society often sees weight as a variable directly linked to perceptions of health. Height, on the other hand, is accepted because it's based on genetics and is unchangeable.

Confidence beyond the measuring tape: Ever found yourself on tiptoes in front of the mirror, wishing you were a few inches taller? Or maybe you opted for flats instead of heels because you didn't want to tower over everyone? We seldom seem to be just the right height. But the reality is that height is a fixed attribute with limited scope for change. Yes, visual strategies such as posture, colors, patterns, or choice of footwear can subtly influence the perception of height, but the intrinsic value of leadership isn't measured in inches any more than it is in pounds.

Nevertheless, tall leaders are often seen as commanding, assertive, and more competent than their shorter counterparts, yet tall leaders often struggle with assumptions that they might be intimidating or unapproachable. In contrast, shorter leaders may be seen as dynamic, agile, and approachable, yet they face stereotypes that say they may lack authority or be less capable than their taller counterparts. These dynamics of height—or lack of it—are especially evident in hierarchical environments like the military or public service where height can subtly influence perceptions of command and capability. And for those leaders who represent their agencies in public, height becomes a factor in settings where they are photographed or filmed alongside others. Taller leaders may unconsciously dominate group photos or televised events, which can affect how their stature is perceived relative to those next to them. Shorter leaders can easily be overshadowed. You may never seem to be just the right height. So let's see if research provides any insightful correlations between height and leadership perception.

Sylvia Ann Hewlett and her team surveyed college-educated professionals and senior executives about executive presence. They found women are judged more critically by their weight, whereas men are more likely to be judged by their height.

Of those surveyed, 16 percent said it's important for men to be tall compared to just 6 percent for women. According to Nancy M. Blaker and her research team, this "height premium" exists in particular across domains like politics, business, and the military. Daniel E. Re and his research team even found that, in corporate settings, taller CEOs are rated as more competent leaders by employees, and their companies achieve higher profits.

In fact, significant amounts of research show that height can be helpful in terms of perceived authority and your professional identity. But it's crucial to remember that, although being tall might influence how others perceive your leadership potential, height doesn't automatically make you a more effective leader. The perception of tall leaders is based more on stereotypes than on any real evidence that height enhances leadership skills.

So what does define a leader in service and duty? It's certainly not the number on a scale or on a measuring tape. It's the ability to embrace your unique physical attributes and to leverage them so you can lead with confidence. A strong professional identity transcends physical dimensions because, in the end, the real measure of your professional identity isn't found in your weight or height but in the confidence you project. It's about being unapologetically yourself and owning your presence in every room you walk into, whether it's a town hall meeting, courtroom, or community event.

Leaders Are Confident about Their Age

In France we have a special appreciation for both young and aged wines and cheeses. Young wines and cheeses are fresh and vibrant, bringing a burst of energy and straightforward flavors to the table. They bring an immediate, joyous experience and remind us of enthusiasm and innovation. There's a sense of celebration and anticipation with young wines, as they often mark new beginnings and seasonal transitions. In contrast, aged wines and cheeses are celebrated for their depth, complexity, and richness.

They symbolize wisdom, experience, and nuanced understanding. They tell endless stories through their flavor and offer a depth of experience and a richness of character that only time can develop. You may be thinking, *Sure but the French would use any excuse to consume wine and cheese.* And, in most cases, you'd be right. But there's more to my point.

Just as each wine and cheese has its unique qualities at a certain age, so does each stage of our professional identity. Whether you're at the beginning of your public service career or have decades of experience, your age is an asset that brings its own distinct value to the sector.

Age, like height but unlike weight, is an immutable number, a marker of time. But contrary to popular belief, age has no direct correlation with success. Across the spectrum of history and into the modern era leaders have emerged at various stages of their lives, showcasing that age is not a determinant of capability. Luckily, success is age agnostic in the public sector.

Embrace the vibrancy of youth: You might be one of the younger service and duty leaders lauded for your agility, both mentally and physically. You're often seen as the vanguard of innovation, bringing fresh perspectives from recent education and a zeal for progressive methodologies in government operations, community engagement, or technology integration. Your age represents a drive for momentum and an ambition to innovate and expand the horizons of your respective field.

Harness the wisdom of experience: Or you could be that seasoned public leader whose years are viewed as a compendium of expertise, a living library of knowledge and experience garnered through years of dedication and hands-on work in policy-making, public safety, or civic administration. Your age is often associated with a profound understanding and a reassuring presence that commands respect in any professional challenge.

Nevertheless, our age also bears a psychological weight, influencing both our self-perception and the expectations of those we work with and serve. In the public sector, where leaders operate in a constant spotlight, assumptions and expectations tied to age can feel particularly amplified.

Younger leaders may face skepticism about their ability to navigate complex systems. Similarly, younger leaders in uniformed roles, such as law enforcement or the military, may find it challenging to establish authority in environments where seniority often equates to respect. Meanwhile, their public-facing counterparts might struggle to gain credibility with older constituencies who may view their ideas as too progressive or untested.

For older leaders the challenges take on a different form. In a fast-changing world they might encounter assumptions about their adaptability or proficiency with emerging technologies—perceptions that unfairly undermine their expertise and strategic insight. In high-stress or crisis situations, older leaders may face unspoken doubts about their physical stamina or ability to make quick decisions, despite their extensive experience in similar scenarios. Even their vast knowledge is sometimes reframed as a marker of the past rather than an asset for the future with team members and the public leaning on them more as mentors than active decision-makers. These age-related biases often create unique pressures, especially in roles requiring visible leadership or public engagement. The media, for instance, can amplify these perceptions, framing younger leaders as inexperienced upstarts or older leaders as outdated figures clinging to tradition.

And we may even have found our own age casting some shadows of self-doubt from time to time. Haven't we all, at some point in our youth, tried to look older to fit in or be taken more seriously? Maybe some of us borrowed our parent's blazer or practiced our "serious face" in the mirror before that big interview. Others might have added a few years to their age on a dating profile or tried to sneak into a bar before they were legal. And then, as the years went by, the script flipped. Suddenly, some of us found ourselves tempted to knock a few years off our age, investing in that miracle

anti-aging cream, or choosing outfits that scream "youthful and trendy" to prove we've still got it.

It's human nature to wish to be perceived as younger or older, but challenges often arise when efforts to alter your age's perception go to extremes. Excessive attempts, such as dressing overly younger or older, extreme dieting or fitness regimens that are unsustainable, the use of heavy makeup to conceal natural features, the adoption of fashion trends that don't align with our personal style or age, or overindulgence in plastic surgery can convey a lack of confidence in our natural progression. These efforts, despite aiming to enhance our appearance may, instead, project a sense of insecurity and often backfire. When leaders resort to extreme measures to alter their age appearance, it can overshadow their competencies and achievements. It's a delicate balance between using visual elements to slightly improve your confidence and adjust your age's perception and overstepping into the territory where those elements detract from your authenticity as a leader in service and duty.

Instead, for younger public leaders, the focus should be on leveraging the fresh perspectives, energy, and adaptability that come with youth. It's about demonstrating a willingness to learn, innovate, and bring new ideas to the table. It involves using your unique insights and enthusiasm to drive change and inspire others, proving that age is just a number and that potential and capability in public service are not confined by years. Seasoned public leaders should establish their age-appropriate professional identity, capitalizing on the strengths that come with their experience while challenging any perceived constraints associated with their age.

The key to navigating age is, once again, embracing it. Owning your years with confidence means celebrating milestones and viewing your age as an asset, not a barrier. Present yourself in a way that highlights the intrinsic value and the unique perspective you bring to your professional role. Remember, it's not the number of years that define your professional identity but the quality and impact of your contributions. Your age is just a number.

Leaders Are Confident about Their Gender Identity

It will come as no surprise that gender dynamics play a significant role in leadership perceptions. Hold on, gentlemen! If you're thinking of skipping this chapter, please reconsider. Navigating gender dynamics is a critical skill for every leader in service and duty, regardless of gender.

Traditionally, nurturing roles were seen as women's work, whereas positions of authority were for men. But today's professional world of public service is challenging those stereotypes and, often, changing them. Even though we've made progress, subtle shades of those stereotypes linger, showing up in the biases and expectations that remain embedded in our workplace culture. We need an ongoing effort to root them out as we continue moving toward an equitable professional environment.

Women leaders have shattered ceilings, but invisible barriers still hold them back. Sure, many barriers to gender equity have been broken down, often under public scrutiny that forces government agencies to change. But the subtler, less visible forms of inequality still chip away at true equity. These biases are harder to spot and even harder to tackle because they're deeply woven into workplace cultures and attitudes. Thus, women in leadership still have to navigate these gender-based perceptions, making sure their work's quality is the main focus, not their gender.

For women in leadership, expectations often feel like a double-edged sword. On the one hand they are celebrated as symbols of progress, but on the other their decisions are frequently overanalyzed. In roles traditionally dominated by men—such as law enforcement or national defense—women leaders may find their authority questioned more readily while their leadership style is subjected to heightened scrutiny. Walking the fine line between being approachable and authoritative is a balancing act many female leaders still must navigate daily.

Let's see what the research says about these gender dynamics. Janice Fanning Madden at the University of Pennsylvania highlighted an imbalance in teams within large firms. In places where income is tied to performance and commission, women, despite showing equal skills, were often given accounts with less potential than the accounts given to their male counterparts. Similarly, research from Joanna Barsh and Lareina Yee at McKinsey & Company confirmed invisible barriers are holding women back more than overt sexism is.

The "Howard vs. Heidi" case study by Frank Flynn at Columbia Business School is particularly revealing. Participants were asked to evaluate a candidate profile, identical except for the name: Howard for one group and Heidi for the other. Howard was seen as competent, effective, and likable with people eager to work with him. Heidi, despite being seen as competent and effective, wasn't met with the same warmth or enthusiasm. This shows gender bias: high-achieving women often face a stricter social ledger in which their success might actually reduce their likability—something their male counterparts don't face as often.

Charles M. Futrell, in a study published in the *Journal of Personal Selling and Sales Management*, found similar biases. Professionals assessed leadership styles on video, and their evaluations were heavily influenced by the manager's gender, regardless of the leadership approach. Unconscious gender biases made the same behaviors seem more or less effective, depending on whether the manager was a woman or a man.

The key to overcoming these stereotypes is to embrace your gender identity with confidence and showcase your unique leadership style. This means not feeling pressured to fit into traditional leadership modes.

By cultivating a leadership identity that includes both empathy and assertiveness, you can redefine what it means to lead with influence and integrity, regardless of gender.

Gender bias has no boundaries; it affects everyone. We often talk about gender bias in terms of women and race in terms of people of color. But what about the other groups? Defined by narrow interpretations of masculinity, men also are pressured to be decisive, tough, and unyielding, leaving little room for vulnerability or emotional openness. These standards, drilled into us from a young age through family, education, and media can be just as restrictive and damaging to team members in public service roles as any other bias.

In leadership, these pressures manifest in various ways. Male leaders might feel the need to adopt an overly aggressive style, believing that showing any hesitation or uncertainty could be seen as weakness. They might avoid asking for help or feedback, fearing it might undermine their image of competence and control. During negotiations the pressure to be tough can lead to missed opportunities for collaboration and compromise, and the constant need to project confidence can stop male leaders from expressing doubts or discussing challenges openly, which can stifle growth and innovation. In public-facing leadership, this creates a challenge: How do you remain relatable to the community you serve while projecting the decisiveness expected of those in positions of authority?

True equality means understanding that these constraints affect all genders. This includes nonbinary and transgender leaders who are navigating a world that's still learning to understand and accept gender beyond the binary. Their visibility in leadership roles is itself an act of courage and representation. For nonbinary and transgender leaders, the challenge is often about being seen and respected for their professional capabilities first without their gender identity overshadowing their skills and contributions.

They might face inappropriate questions or comments about their gender identity, diverting attention from their professional message. Their authority might be questioned or undermined due to biases or a lack of understanding. Or they may find public forums or events dominated by traditional gender norms, making it difficult to build relationships on an equal footing.

Instead of being evaluated purely on merit, their gender identity can often become a focal point in media coverage, overshadowing their professional achievements. Headlines and narratives may emphasize their identity over the depth of their contributions, creating a disproportionate focus that detracts from their leadership capabilities. This heightened visibility in the media not only diverts attention, it also can amplify biases or invite unwarranted public commentary. Additionally, navigating administrative systems not yet fully inclusive of nonbinary or transgender identities—such as outdated forms or uniform standards—adds another layer of complexity, even in roles where equity and inclusivity are central values.

By focusing on professional acumen and advocating for environments where everyone is evaluated based on their abilities and contributions, we can help ensure leadership in government and public service is defined by the quality of work, not by gender identity. We can all play a role in pushing for policies and norms that honor gender diversity by embodying empathetic and inclusive leadership. Alongside these efforts it's crucial to recognize how gender bias can still subtly shape our interactions and workplace culture through unspoken microaggressions.

Embracing your gender identity as part of your leadership is a profound statement of confidence and acceptance that sets a powerful example. The key lies in being comfortable in your own skin and using your unique experiences to inform and enhance your leadership approach beyond your gender. At the core of your professional reputation should always be an unwavering commitment to excellence and the quality of leadership you express. In such environments, gender becomes one of many aspects of a leader's identity—not a hurdle to overcome but a facet that enriches your perspective.

For you, this means harmonizing your external presence with your inner identity, ensuring your professional identity reflects both your competence and your authenticity. Let your gender identity enhance, not define, your leadership style.

Leaders Are Confident about Their Style

Do you have a style icon, someone who always seems to get it right, effortlessly blending consistency and creativity, someone who wears the same confidence every day, yet always looks fresh and different? They have that certain je ne sais quoi—a flair that makes heads turn and a presence that lingers long after they've left the room.

Confession time: my style icon is Iris Apfel. If you've ever seen Iris, you'll remember her for her oversized glasses, chunky jewelry, and flamboyant prints. She fascinates me. Her style is bold, unapologetic, and uniquely hers. Would you ever find me dressed like Iris? No, first because it's her style, not mine, and second, because my environment doesn't allow for such flamboyance. This is the heart of one of our everyday challenges: embracing ourselves yet accepting that not all things are possible if you interact in a professional environment that doesn't match your personal approach.

Yet even in public service environments there's plenty of room to weave in distinctive elements that set your style apart. You might be thinking, *But I wear a uniform. Does style even apply to me?* The answer is a resounding *yes*. While uniforms may limit your options in terms of some choices, they don't restrict your ability to exhibit personal style. Style is about more than just what you wear; it's about how you wear it. It's reflected in your grooming, your posture, and the care you take to maintain your appearance. Even within the confines of a uniform, the way you carry yourself, your choice of subtle accessories (if allowed), and your attention to detail can communicate volumes about your personal identity. And let's not forget there are times when you won't be in uniform, when your personal style will play a crucial role in how you're perceived. The principles that follow are just as relevant to those moments as they are to your professional role. The key is balance: Your style should never overshadow your competencies but complement and enhance your professional narrative. This means understanding what style is not as much as what it is.

Style isn't about mimicking others. It's about discovering your own unique expression. It's not about seeking validation from others; it's about feeling empowered and comfortable in your own choices.

Style isn't just about color or fit. It's about the message you want to send, rooted in the values you want to project—confidence, approachability, authority, trustworthiness, or dedication—and how they are encapsulated in your visual presence. It's a broader expression of your identity and offers a glimpse into your personality without uttering a single word.

Style isn't about chasing the whims of fashion or flaunting the price tags of luxury brands. It's not about squeezing into the latest silhouette or echoing the masses. It's about embracing timeless elegance and quality that reflect your personal values and essence.

Style doesn't demand perfection. It's not a one-size-fits-all formula. It's not about dressing to impress others or putting on a costume for approval. True style transcends trends and societal expectations; it's an individual expression that remains steady, unaffected by public opinion.

In the public sector your style acts as a visual signature, making you easily recognizable and memorable. Here, mastering your style means understanding that going overboard can be counterproductive. It's not about pushing boundaries to the extreme but pushing them just enough to be intriguing and, above all, true to yourself. Because your style shouldn't distract; it should fascinate. It shouldn't raise questions; it should assert confidence in your role as a leader.

It could be the elegance of a custom-tailored suit for a legislative session, the strategic selection of an accessory that reflects your agency's ethos, or the timeless charm of a subtle yet polished piece of jewelry that complements your role in public service.

It's in the carefully chosen pin on your lapel symbolizing your department's mission, the glimpse of an unexpected pattern on a tie that hints at your creative approach to community engagement, or the deliberate choice of a sleek briefcase signaling a meticulous eye for detail in a field where details matter. These elements shouldn't scream for attention but invite intrigue and respect.

Defining your personal style can be challenging. Unlike pursuing a specific role or niche in your public service career, which may be influenced by passion, skill, or opportunity, style is more abstract and deeply personal. You must engage in an introspective process to determine how you want to present yourself and be perceived by the world in your leadership role.

The question, "What's your style?" can often leave professionals pondering. Style is complex and requires many questions to be answered before you can confidently define it. Here are some of those questions:

- Does your style amplify your voice?
- How does your style make you feel about yourself?
- How does it affect your confidence?
- Are there unique elements that make you memorable?
- Does your style incorporate elements of your personality?
- Can it evolve while maintaining your core identity?
- Does it reflect your leadership capabilities?
- How does your style influence your team's perception?
- Is it practical and functional for your daily activities?
- How does your style align with your agency's values and culture?
- How does your style adapt to different contexts?
- How does your style bridge or speak to diverse stakeholder backgrounds?
- How do your style choices reflect your commitment to quality and attention to detail?

Only by answering these questions can you begin to craft a style narrative that is unique and that aligns with your best self, leading to a style and professional identity that consistently and coherently communicates who you are at your core as a leader in service and duty. It's about selecting pieces that enhance your visual presence and resonate with who you are, your values, and the message you wish to convey. This journey might be challenging, but the result is a style that genuinely reflects your inner self and professional ethos.

There is no shortcut to developing a sense of style. The key is finding ways to express your public sector zeal and personalized flair through intentional choices that enhance, not distract. It's about cultivating a coherent, intentional style alignment between individual, agency, and institutional image without compromising taste or propriety.

By avoiding heavy-handed themes, leaders in service and duty demonstrate they have a nuanced understanding of embodying their agency's identity with polish and self-assuredness while letting genuine passion and expertise shine through in elegant yet impactful ways.

So take the time to explore and refine your personal style. Wear it with confidence and pride. Let it reflect the leader you are and the impact you aim to make in your agency or the broader public sector. Your style is uniquely yours. Own it and let it shine as a reflection of the exceptional leader in service and duty you are.

Chapter 4
Leaders Look Authentic

The Art of Standing Out
While Fitting In
Without Disappearing.

Chapter 4: Leaders Look Authentic

Let's venture once again into the fascinating world of animals and take a look at two other remarkable creatures: First, picture a chameleon. This little reptile with its googly eyes and color-changing skin is nature's ultimate shapeshifter. It can blend seamlessly into any environment, from lush green leaves to sandy deserts. It's not just hiding; it's communicating, regulating temperature, and surviving. The chameleon is a master of adaptation. But here's the catch: In all that blending, its true self is often hidden beneath those shifting colors, rarely showing its genuine hues.

Now picture a peacock. With its dazzling feathers and extravagant display, the peacock is all about showing off. It struts around, flaunting its stunning array of colors for everyone to see. The peacock doesn't blend in, it stands out, boldly and unapologetically. Its showy display screams health, vitality, and confidence. But although the peacock's feathers attract admiration, they also make it an easy target for predators.

In the professional world, leaders face similar dilemmas. Should they be like the chameleon, blending in and adapting to every situation, or like the peacock, boldly displaying their true selves? Being a chameleon means constantly adjusting your professional identity to fit various contexts and expectations. This adaptability can be a great asset, especially in diverse and dynamic public service environments.

But there's a downside: you might lose sight of your true self. When you're always changing to match your surroundings, there's a risk your unique contributions will become overshadowed by your desire to fit in.

On the flip side, being a peacock means showcasing your true self with confidence and flair. This approach can make you memorable and earn you respect for your individuality and courage. But there's a catch here too: In professional settings that value conformity and predictability, being too much of a peacock can make you seem out of touch. It's easy to be seen as more concerned with making statements than with achieving your agency's goals. So how do you strike the right balance?

The pursuit of authenticity has become a rallying cry for leaders across all industries, including the public sector. But what does it mean to be an authentic leader in today's high-stakes environment? Is it about unfiltered self-expression, or is there a more nuanced approach that balances personal identity with professional expectations?

At its core, being authentic means being true to your own personality, spirit, or character. Yet it's a concept that's far more nuanced than simply "being yourself."

Ignoring your environment and the context in which you operate can lead to a dangerous misconception about authenticity, one that's especially prevalent in the advice, "You do you." This notion suggests being authentic means you can do, say, or wear whatever you want, regardless of the situation. It's advice that, admittedly, many of us, including myself, have given as well as received.

But this advice fails to recognize the importance of aligning your authentic self with the expectations and norms of your professional setting. When you disregard the context and operate solely on the you do you principle, you risk coming across as tone-deaf or even disrespectful, which can be a costly mistake in a sector built on service and public trust. It can give the detrimental impression that you don't care about anyone or anything, anywhere, at any time.

Authenticity isn't an excuse to disregard norms. The reality is that authenticity does not exist in a vacuum. Just as the chameleon adapts to its environment while maintaining its essence, leaders in service and duty operate within a complex network of relationships, expectations, and social norms. Although it's important to stay true to your essence, you also must recognize that your self-expression has an impact on those around you, including your team and the public you serve. Using authenticity as a justification for ignoring any and all professional norms risks damaging the very relationships and trust that are essential to success as a leader in service and duty. When you disregard these norms in the name of authenticity, you can come across as unprofessional, untrustworthy, or even arrogant, perceptions that can severely undermine your effectiveness.

For instance, military leaders often operate within strict codes of conduct so that even slight deviations from established norms can be seen as undermining authority or institutional discipline. Leaders in community-focused agencies may find their authenticity is evaluated not just by their teams but by the public they serve, which often holds them to higher ethical standards. In such environments, projecting authenticity means balancing personal expression with a commitment to the expectations of a broader, more diverse audience. Failing to strike this balance may lead to public misinterpretation or loss of trust, especially when leaders represent agencies built on accountability and service. This fact doesn't mean you need to completely suppress your individuality. Rather, it means you need to find a way to express your authentic self within the framework of your professional context.

There's no such thing as a singular authentic self. The notion that we each have one "authentic self"—sorry to break the news—is a lie. Just like the chameleon, we need to adapt to numerous roles. We're parents, siblings, children, friends, neighbors, and colleagues as well as leaders in service and duty. Each of these roles demands a different facet of our presentation. Imagine interacting with your children in the same way as with your constituents,

speaking to your parents as you would to your senior leaders, or wearing your gym outfit to a town hall meeting. Although there may be a consistent thread of core values and beliefs that define you, the expression of your authenticity must vary, depending on the situation.

Authenticity, then, is not about rigid adherence to a single, unchanging self in all contexts. The focus is on being true to your core values while possessing the flexibility to effectively navigate various environments.

Those in uniformed services, for example, should maintain an authoritative and disciplined demeanor in public while being approachable and empathetic within their teams. Similarly, leaders in highly visible agencies must navigate the delicate line between projecting professionalism and remaining relatable to community members. Doing so requires an exceptional level of adaptability—whether addressing a press conference, leading a team meeting, or engaging with constituents—so that each role is an opportunity to align authenticity with audience expectations.

In leadership, this means finding harmony between your private persona and your professional identity, ensuring each role you play is infused with your values. It's not about concealing who you are; it's about respectfully acknowledging the part you play in each aspect and role of your life and doing so with sincerity and professionalism.

Authenticity is not a fixed state. Many professionals believe that once they discover their authentic self, they're set for life. They think authenticity is a destination. But the truth is authenticity is a journey, not a final stop.

As we navigate through our careers and our lives, we are constantly growing, learning, and evolving. Our experiences shape us, our relationships change us, and our perspectives shift. As a result, our understanding of ourselves and how we express our authenticity also should evolve. What felt authentic to us in our twenties may not feel the same way in our forties or sixties.

Peacocks don't develop their striking tail feathers right away. When they're born, peachicks are covered in a dull, brown plumage that provides camouflage and protection from predators. It takes years to develop their characteristic tail feathers, and their colors continue to change as they mature.

For leaders in service and duty, evolving authenticity is often tied to the dynamic nature of their roles. Consider a government official who transitions from community engagement to legislative duties or a military leader who moves from active combat roles to administrative leadership. Their expression of authenticity must evolve to suit those shifts while staying true to their core values. The adaptability required in the public sector is amplified by the constant public and media scrutiny, making self-awareness and the ability to refine their authenticity over time not just a choice but a necessity.

You need to regularly reassess and adjust your authentic expression. You need to take the time to check in with yourself to ask if the way you're presenting yourself to the world still aligns with your core values and the evolving demands. It's a process of continuous self-discovery and self-alignment, one that means recognizing that what made us authentic leaders in the past may not be what makes us authentic leaders in the present or future.

Authenticity is not an excuse to be unfiltered. There's a common misconception that to be authentic you must share every detail of your life and thoughts, holding nothing back. But this couldn't be further from the truth, especially in public service where discretion and professionalism are highly valued.

Think about the peacock again. Its bold display is carefully chosen, and not everything is on show at all times. Authenticity is about being true to yourself, but it doesn't mean you have to reveal every aspect of your life to everyone. Instead, authenticity is about being transparent about the things that matter while maintaining appropriate boundaries. For example, community leaders may find their personal lives scrutinized by the public or media, but oversharing can lead to distractions or misunderstandings.

At the same time, uniformed team members, such as those in the military or law enforcement, often operate under a heightened expectation of discretion so that even minor lapses in communication can have significant consequences. Maintaining authenticity while navigating these pressures requires a nuanced approach in which transparency is balanced with professionalism, ensuring trust without oversharing.

These boundaries are often crafted by the implicit expectations and unspoken scripts that permeate every public sector role and society at large. Like invisible guardrails, they guide and shape perceptions, influencing how others view and interpret your actions, words, and appearance. Society has preconceived notions of what a leader in service and duty should look like, sound like, and act like. These notions, while rarely explicitly stated, carry significant weight in how your authenticity is perceived and received, and your visual appearance can either confirm or challenge these notions.

During my keynotes I present participants with various images of individuals dressed in professional attire. I then pose a question: "Which of these individuals would you entrust with your legal battles, your computer setup, or the education of your children?" The responses are predictably consistent, underscoring how quickly we form perceptions based solely on someone's visual appearance. My audiences' inner dialogue might go something like this: *The sharp lines of that charcoal-gray suit, the impeccable white shirt, and the red tie exude a strategic and respectable presence. That has to be the lawyer.* Right next to that person is someone in smart casual attire—a coat, a light shirt without a tie, and slacks. *Clearly, that's the IT expert.* Then there's someone in a light, pastel dress that flows softly, the kind that suggests kindness and a nurturing spirit: *Surely, that's the teacher.*

Every time my audience seems surprised that they share the same opinions. Once again they might think it's witchcraft. But the reality is much simpler: I'm just tapping into and leveraging the preexisting scripts in their minds.

It's not magic; it's the power of subconscious visual cues and deeply ingrained stereotypes. Let's dive into these mental scripts and see which ones you might be adhering to or have internalized. Understanding these patterns can empower you to strategically align your professional identity with your authentic self.

Keywords Are the Keys to Authenticity

Every sector has a mental "uniform"—a sartorial standard that might not be as overt and codified as for a restaurant chef, a hotel concierge, a spa therapist, a tour guide or, in your case, a police officer, a firefighter, or a member of the military, but it's implicitly understood. These are the "perceived uniforms," the unspoken dress codes shaped by societal expectations and assumptions about certain professions. These perceived uniforms serve as a visual shorthand, helping to forge an immediate connection between professional identity and public perception. Although they are complex in their detail, I simplify them by applying keywords to these mental uniforms.

"So what are the expected keywords in my sector and for my mental uniform?" you ask. The answer lies in the collective expectations of all stakeholders—team members, colleagues, senior leaders, constituents, media, or the general public—who interact with you. These keywords become the essence of your perceived uniform. By carefully crafting a professional identity that aligns with these keywords, you can construct a perception that not only meets professional standards but also resonates with the unique characteristics of your field in the public sector, thereby reinforcing your role and strengthening your personal identity.

Cracking your sector's keyword and your profession's DNA: The first step to crafting your personal and professional style is to identify the keywords associated with your specific role or sector. These keywords encapsulate the core values, traits, and expectations that define success in your field of public service.

To determine your sector's or profession's keywords, please consider the following questions:

- What are the primary goals and objectives in your role?
- What are the core values that underpin your sector?
- What are the most significant trends shaping your field in public service?
- What are the unique contributions or impacts expected in your role?
- What expectations do constituents, team members, and senior leaders have of professionals in your role?
- What phrases are commonly used to describe your sector in media, public discussions, or strategic plans?
- What qualities do the most influential figures in your sector embody?

By reflecting on these questions and observing the norms and standards within your sector, you can begin to identify the keywords that define your role's perceived uniform.

Defining your distinctive edge and personal keyword: The most authentic leaders understand that they can convey a narrative about who they are through their visual presence, and they're clear about the keywords that describe this narrative. Each keyword tells a part of their story, and each look confirms its essence.

If your professional ethos is grounded in dependability, integrity, and commitment to public service, your professional identity should reinforce those qualities visually. Alternatively, if you pride yourself on being innovative, bold, and a visionary in government or community leadership, your visual choices might be more creative and modern, reflecting a forward-thinking mindset.

Have you considered the unique traits that define you in your role and how they translate into the visual messages you wish to instantly imprint? This is the most crucial step because it allows you to pinpoint a style that not only makes you feel confident but also conveys the key messages you intend to communicate with your professional identity.

Harmonizing your sector's expectations and your personal essence: Once your sector's keyword and your personal keywords are established, the next phase is alignment—that is, checking whether these keywords echo and resonate with the ethos of your public service profession. If you're fortunate, the keywords you selected to describe yourself align with the persona expected in your professional sphere. When there's a match, it can feel like a natural extension of your identity. Conversely, if there's a disconnect, it can manifest as a nagging sense of being out of place, prompting you to question why you feel like you don't belong in your role.

Such leaders in service and duty often find themselves at a crossroads, grappling with the tension between their authentic selves and the expectations of their roles. They may feel like they're constantly putting on a mask, suppressing parts of themselves to fit into a mold that doesn't quite fit. This internal dissonance can lead to feelings of frustration, burnout, and even loss of purpose.

On the flip side, when leaders in service and duty achieve alignment between their keywords, they tend to thrive. They exude a sense of ease and confidence in their roles, as if they were born to do what they do. Their authenticity shines through effortlessly, and they have a way of inspiring and motivating others simply by being themselves. This alignment allows them to bring their whole selves to their work, tapping into a deep well of intrinsic motivation and passion. They don't feel the need to compartmentalize or hide parts of themselves because their authentic identity is not just accepted but celebrated.

Emerging from the myriads of possible keywords and attributes are seven distinct perception personas. Each of these personas is like a unique flavor that represents a specific set of values and traits professionals either embody naturally or are expected to adopt in their roles. But here's the thing: These personas go far beyond just clothing choices. They represent the holistic professional identity that leaders are expected to uphold in their work and interactions. The seven personas can be categorized into two types—your primary persona and your secondary persona.

- **Your primary persona** is like your professional backbone, akin to your DNA and the core of your identity. It's reflected in the consistent threads of your character, influencing your instinctive choices and the way you inherently engage.

- **Your secondary persona** is more fluid and adaptable, sculpted by the ebb and flow of your external experiences, age, education, preferences, and the continuous curve of personal and professional development. It grants you the flexibility to adapt, to mold your choices to fit the myriads of scenarios you encounter throughout your career and life.

Whereas your primary persona remains steadfast, your secondary persona acts as a versatile sidekick. It doesn't overshadow your core; instead, it enhances it, allowing you a wider range of expression. Together, they form a cohesive identity that's both true to your essence and attuned to the nuances of your professional environment.

Before we jump into outlining the specific personas, it's crucial to understand that they are not rigid boxes. They're more than just labels. They influence our perspective on the world and, consequently, these personas often manifest in our external presentation in the clothes we choose, the hairstyles we adopt, and the accessories we select. All of these are outward expressions of our inner narrative. And you might find yourself resonating with more than one primary or secondary persona, but we'll address that complexity later.

It's also important to recognize that, although I use elements of each persona's visual appearance to describe them, their traits permeate into behavior, communication, digital presence, and environment. These personas are holistic, encompassing not just how leaders look but how they act, interact, and present themselves in all aspects of their professional and personal lives.

But it's often through our visual appearance that we receive the first strong indication of how these personas express their unique keywords. Their looks serve as the initial canvas upon which they paint the picture of who they are and what they stand for. Their visual appearance is like the opening scene in the movie of their professional identity, setting the tone and creating expectations for the interactions to come. But just like in a movie, their story goes beyond the opening scene. Their visual presence is just the beginning. It's through their actions, words, and the way they engage with the world around them that the full depth and complexity of their persona is revealed. So considering all of this, are you ready to explore the three primary personas?

The Explorer: Approachable and Relaxed

Explorers embody a spirit that is both adventurous and pragmatic, often reflected in a style that prioritizes comfort and practicality.

They choose their wardrobe less for the latest fashion trends and more for the functionality and durability of the garments. Imagine their attire as ready for an impromptu location visit as it is for a team meeting—comfortable slacks paired with a resilient button-down shirt and sturdy footwear that speaks to a life in motion.

In their wardrobe you'll find many earthy tones that serve a purpose: utility jackets with pockets aplenty, fabrics that can withstand the elements, and colors that blend with the natural world.

They have a preference for clothing that endures the wear and tear of their adventures without demanding meticulous care.

Their approach to body image is straightforward and unpretentious. Their physique, whether it's conditioned by active pursuits or carries the robustness of a life well lived, is a testament to their experiences rather than a curated image. In their world the body is less a canvas for fashion and more a vessel for adventure, a mindset that brings a unique confidence and an unbothered attitude toward societal beauty standards.

When it comes to grooming, the Explorer favors a minimalistic approach, if any. A touch of moisturizer for a healthy glow, a swipe of clear lip balm, and a simple hair style are all they need to maintain their natural look, ready for whatever the day may bring.

Their accessories, like the sporty watch on their wrist or the durable briefcase slung over their shoulder, are chosen for resilience and utility, echoing the Explorer's readiness for life's spontaneous adventures.

For hair and nails, the Explorer opts for easy maintenance, prioritizing health and manageability. A simple, practical haircut suits their active lifestyle. Their manicure and pedicure are neat yet unfussy, often favoring clear polish or natural tones that don't show wear easily.

- **Keyword:** comfort
- **Perceived traits:** active, adventurous, casual, approachable, optimistic, energetic, natural, direct, spontaneous, enthusiastic
- **Perceived challenges:** disorganized, dull, graceless, mannerless, ordinary, unambitious, unpolished, weak

This persona shines in roles that value utility, approachability, and an active presence in the field. In the public sector Explorers are well suited for a role such as a community outreach specialist where the Explorer's approachable and enthusiastic nature to effectively engage with diverse groups is invaluable. Similarly, for public health field workers the Explorer's active and energetic style enables them to navigate complex, real-world scenarios with resilience and clarity. Or for urban planners focused on sustainability projects, the Explorer's pragmatic and forward-thinking approach is key to implementing green initiatives, managing stakeholder relationships, and envisioning future-ready solutions that balance innovation with practicality.

As a park ranger the Explorer's adventurous spirit and hands-on approach make them invaluable in roles that require both physical stamina and interpersonal skills.

Their down-to-earth demeanor fosters trust among visitors, making them relatable and effective. Or, in disaster response coordination the Explorer's ability to remain calm under pressure and adapt quickly to ever-changing circumstances is essential.

Explorers thrive as Special Operations Officers in the military where their adventurous spirit and ability to adapt to changing environments make them indispensable in dynamic missions requiring quick thinking and physical resilience. In law enforcement they excel as Community Policing Officers where their approachable demeanor and enthusiasm help build trust and strong connections with diverse communities, fostering collaboration and safety.

On the flip side, Explorers might find it challenging to thrive in roles that demand a high level of formality or strict adherence to traditional protocols. For instance, positions that prioritize rigid hierarchy or that require a polished and refined professional identity—such as high-level diplomatic roles or formal administrative positions—may clash with the Explorer's preference for flexibility and pragmatism. In such environments their relaxed style might be perceived as too casual or unstructured, potentially hindering their ability to gain trust and authority.

The Traditionalist: Trustworthy and Reliable

The Traditionalist carries an air of timeless elegance, exuding a commitment to enduring styles that is immediately apparent. They aren't swayed by passing trends but are firmly rooted in classic principles.

Envision them in attire that pays homage to the past while fitting impeccably into the present: a well-tailored suit that defies the ebb and flow of fads, a crisp dress shirt that whispers decades of sophistication, or leather shoes polished to perfection.

In their wardrobe you'll discover a carefully selected ensemble that defies the transient whims of fashion. Each item is tended to meticulously, ensuring their presentation is flawless as it honors their conservative sensibilities.

Their perspective on body image is in harmony with this classic sense of style. The Traditionalist adopts a manner that conveys diligent self-care and a refined composure, regardless of their body type. Their physique reflects a devotion to a persona that upholds their values—subtle yet unmistakably dignified.

When it comes to grooming, the Traditionalist opts for the timeless: a neat hairstyle, a clean shave or well-trimmed facial hair, and a subtle fragrance that serves as a tribute to poise rather than as a pursuit of the spotlight.

Their accessories are chosen with discretion, from the understated elegance of their cufflinks to the classic lines of their wristwatch. As for hair and nail care, they select styles that stand the test of time—perhaps a sleek side part or a classic manicure.

- **Keyword:** values
- **Perceived traits:** trustworthy, loyal, organized, practical, consistent, dependable, responsible, reliable, conscientious, appropriate
- **Perceived challenges:** authoritarian, boring, conformist, inflexible, elitist, predictable, reserved, uncreative

With their steadfast values and reliability, Traditionalists excel in roles that require trustworthiness, organization, and a commitment to established systems. Thus, traditionalists are well-suited for positions such as a legislative analyst where their conscientious and detail-oriented nature is invaluable in ensuring that laws and policies align with long-term governance goals. Or, as a public sector auditor, the Traditionalist's dependability and adherence to ethical standards ensure thorough and consistent evaluation of financial practices, maintaining transparency and accountability. Their preference for structure and order makes them ideal for roles requiring meticulous planning and execution. Or, as a records management officer, the Traditionalist's methodical approach and commitment to precision ensure the efficient organization and preservation of critical documents, supporting the continuity of institutional memory and compliance with regulations.

Another example is a human resources compliance officer where their practical mindset and reliability allow them to enforce workplace policies and standards effectively, ensuring fair treatment and adherence to legal and ethical guidelines. Or, as a protocol officer, their impeccable sense of tradition and decorum supports the careful orchestration of official events, ensuring every detail upholds the dignity and values of their agency or institution.

Traditionalists are a perfect fit as command sergeant majors in the military where their loyalty, dependability, and organizational skills reinforce discipline and uphold the core values of military tradition. In law enforcement, they shine as Training Academy Instructors, instilling discipline and foundational principles in recruits while embodying a strong sense of tradition and responsibility.

On the flip side, Traditionalists might struggle in roles that demand constant innovation or a break from established norms, such as public relations in fast-evolving digital spaces or crisis management requiring highly flexible responses. Their preference for predictability and structure can hinder their ability to adapt quickly to unconventional challenges or environments that thrive on creativity and spontaneity.

The Cosmopolitan: Sophisticated and Eloquent

The Cosmopolitan is an embodiment of luxury and refinement, a sartorial symphony in which each element harmonizes with their sophisticated lifestyle.

Their wardrobe is a subtle murmur of opulence. Designer brands and lavish pieces are selected not merely for their aesthetic allure but also for their ability to broadcast an air of exclusivity and global sophistication. Their wardrobe maintenance mirrors their dedication to a life well-curated, with each garment receiving the meticulous care needed to maintain its premium appearance.

Their view on body image is anchored in elegance. The Cosmopolitan considers their physique as a canvas for high fashion with each contour gracefully adorned in fine materials.

The manner in which they carry themselves—a synthesis of poise and self-assurance—enhances their impeccable taste in clothing.

When it comes to grooming they strike the perfect balance between understated and impactful, crafting a visage that speaks of refinement and luxury: a perfect hairstyle, a hint of color in their accessories, a subtle fragrance, and a well-manicured appearance that adds just the right touch of sophistication.

Accessories are more than adornments, they're declarations of quality and craftsmanship that articulate their discerning preferences.

Their grooming, including hair and nails, follows the philosophy of "less is more"—as long as it's exquisite. They prefer elegant hairstyles that frame their face and manicures that boast of subtle, neutral tones or classic styles. These choices are intentional, serving not just as aspects of their personal upkeep but as integral parts of their social signature.

Every facet of their appearance, from meticulous skin care routines to the selection of a signature scent, is a conscious act in shaping a professional identity that vibrates with the core of high society.

- **Keyword:** quality
- **Perceived traits:** distinguished, proper, notable, cultivated, refined, meticulous, discerning, dignified, excellent
- **Perceived challenges:** arrogant, bossy, calculating, decadent, impersonal, intolerant, stiff, uncaring

The Cosmopolitan thrives in roles that demand polish, refinement, and a deep understanding of diplomacy and representation. Their distinguished and meticulous persona makes them an asset in positions that require both authority and elegance.

As an ambassador or diplomatic envoy, the Cosmopolitan's discerning taste and ability to project authority enable them to navigate the complexities of international relations with grace.

Their impeccable presentation and composed demeanor foster credibility and build trust in diplomatic circles.

The Cosmopolitan also excels as a government spokesperson where their polished appearance and articulate communication style inspire public confidence. By presenting themselves with dignity and clarity, they can effectively address public concerns, reinforcing trust in their agency.

For those involved in cultural affairs, the Cosmopolitan's refined sense of style and appreciation for diversity allow them to create programs that highlight cultural diplomacy and promote mutual understanding. In addition, Cosmopolitans are well-suited for roles such as public sector strategists where their calculated decision-making and ability to maintain composure in high-pressure environments allow them to effectively shape long-term policies.

Cosmopolitans flourish as military attachés where their polished demeanor, refined communication skills, and global sophistication are critical for fostering international military relations. In law enforcement they excel as Public Affairs Specialists, representing agencies with poise and ensuring their public-facing image resonates with professionalism and quality.

On the other hand, Cosmopolitans might struggle in roles requiring rapid adaptability, hands-on involvement, or informal interactions. For example, positions like disaster relief coordinator or grassroots community organizer may conflict with their preference for structured environments and polished interactions. In such roles their focus on refinement and meticulous planning might come across as inflexible while their preference for exclusivity could be perceived as distant or impersonal.

Remember, there's no right or wrong primary persona: Whether you resonate with the unbound spirit of the Explorer, the steadfast resolve of the Traditionalist, or the sophisticated flair of the Cosmopolitan, each brings its distinctive palette of perceived traits and challenges. But never forget that your primary persona is the quintessence of your being, the inherent nature you carry from the cradle to the crescendo of your career.

It's the unchanging core that defines your authentic self, and it's not something you should attempt to alter.

A Cosmopolitan attempting to mimic the Explorer's casual conduct or an Explorer trying to copy the Traditionalist's formality often will feel uncomfortable, like wearing an ill-fitting garment. This incongruence can radiate subtle cues of inauthenticity that leaves you and others with a sense of dissonance, a feeling that something is amiss, even if you can't pinpoint what it is.

Instead, your adaptability comes from your secondary personas, the versatile facets of your identity that you've honed through experience, environment, and personal and professional development. These are the aspects you can shift and shape. They enable you to purposefully imprint characteristics onto others without sacrificing the integrity of your true self. This is not about changing who you are but about expanding the ways you can showcase yourself to the world.

The Caregiver: Supportive and Nurturing

The Caregiver's style resonates with its delicate finesse. These are the leaders who thread warmth, care, compassion, and nurturing into every interaction.

In their wardrobe you'll find fine, small patterns and soft fabrics that offer comfort both to themselves and those they encounter. Soft colors, such as pastels, are prevalent, reflecting their gentle nature and contributing to a calm atmosphere at all times.

Caregivers curate wardrobes that meld professional expectations with personal touches. Shirts with delicate details, cardigans in soothing hues, and tailored slacks or skirts exemplify their effortless grace. Their clothing is not merely a uniform but a testament to their role as nurturers, blending the demands of their profession with innate compassion.

In their body image the Caregiver appreciates subtlety and health, finding beauty in the natural and the genuine.

Their physical presence is characterized by an understated grace, maintaining a physique that speaks to vitality and genuine care rather than vanity.

For the Caregiver, accessories and personal grooming are reflective of their tender approach to life. Jewelry is minimal and meaningful, shoes are chosen for comfort yet display quiet elegance or small embellishments, and grooming is consistent with their overall ethos—thoughtful and impeccably maintained.

When it comes to grooming, they approach it as they do their role by enhancing features softly and naturally, ensuring their presence is as reassuring as the support they offer.

Their hair is often practical yet inviting, perhaps a soft style or gentle waves, and their nails are clean and neatly groomed, often in muted or clear tones.

- **Keyword:** care
- **Perceived traits:** supportive, caring, warm, nurturing, considerate, compassionate, gentle, soft-spoken, receptive, demure
- **Perceived challenges:** anxious, emotional, dependent, insecure, noncompetitive, naïve, passive, undemanding, hesitant

The Caregiver persona finds its strongest calling in roles that require empathy, connection, and an unwavering dedication to serving the public.

For example, as child welfare case managers, Caregivers use their warmth and attentiveness to advocate for children and families in need. Their ability to connect on a personal level ensures they provide thoughtful solutions while navigating challenging circumstances, fostering hope and stability. In the role of public school counselors, the Caregiver's nurturing demeanor helps students overcome both academic and personal hurdles. By building trust with students, parents, and teachers, they foster an inclusive and supportive school environment that promotes well-being and development.

Community health workers benefit greatly from the Caregiver's natural compassion and ability to connect with diverse populations. Working directly with individuals in underserved areas, they play a crucial role in improving health outcomes by providing education, resources, and personalized care.

As elder care coordinators in public programs, Caregivers apply their organizational and interpersonal skills to create meaningful initiatives for senior citizens. They ensure programs prioritize dignity and quality of life, meeting the unique needs of this population with thoughtful care.

Caregivers are natural military family support specialists, offering compassion and emotional support to service members and their families during deployments and transitions. In law enforcement, they excel as victim advocates where their nurturing and empathetic nature provides essential emotional support and guidance to victims during challenging times.

Caregivers might find themselves at odds with roles that demand intense competition, high-pressure decision-making, or a detached, results-driven approach. Positions such as emergency operations directors or government auditors that require rapid, assertive actions and focus on efficiency over empathy could clash with the Caregiver's natural inclination to prioritize personal connection and understanding. These environments may leave them feeling overwhelmed or unfulfilled.

The Avant-Garde: Individualistic and Creative

The Avant-Garde stands as a testament to their creativity and self-expression, valuable in industries that prize innovation such as interactive media leadership, modern art leadership, or forward-thinking technology leadership.

Their appearance is a vibrant tapestry of artistic exploration with a wardrobe that narrates stories of bold experimentation and the redefining of boundaries.

They select audacious colors, embrace emerging designers, and favor unique silhouettes—the hallmarks of their style—a visual celebration of their commitment to pushing the frontiers of fashion. The maintenance of their wardrobe is an act of artistic devotion, each piece cared for with precision or, sometimes, creatively repurposed in their ongoing narrative.

The Avant-Garde views their physique as a medium for artistic display, embracing a spectrum of styles that challenge conventional beauty norms. They wear their confidence as effortlessly as their eclectic mix of garments, radiating a presence that commands attention and sparks dialogue.

They approach their health with an artistic flair, aligning their physical activities and mental wellness practices with their creative life, even if it means deviating from conventional health routines.

Their accessories, from their statement jewelry to their sculptural shoes, are not mere embellishments but proclamations of their originality, each chosen for its unique design and the conversation it incites.

Their grooming routines are an extension of their creative ethos. Grooming is an opportunity for innovation, and hair and nail care become expressions of their Avant-Garde identity, transcending the typical to become part of their artistic statement. Every element of their appearance is a deliberate choice, a chapter in the creative odyssey they embody, inviting all to witness the living art they present to the world.

- **Keyword:** creativity
- **Perceived traits:** innovative, imaginative, free-spirited, independent, original, unique, unconventional, fearless, impromptu
- **Perceived challenges:** unrealistic, undisciplined, opinionated, neglectful, inconsistent, disruptive, contrary, awkward

The Avant-Garde's unconventional creativity and bold approach make them invaluable in roles that prioritize innovation, independent thinking, and pushing boundaries. As urban development visionaries, Avant-Garde leaders thrive in rethinking city landscapes and designing community spaces that prioritize both functionality and aesthetic appeal. Their fearless creativity inspires innovative approaches to urban challenges, creating vibrant environments that reflect forward-thinking design principles and inclusivity. In the role of public arts program directors the Avant-Garde shines by fostering cultural enrichment and artistic expression within communities. Their originality and ability to champion unconventional ideas ensure the creation of impactful and thought-provoking public art initiatives that resonate with diverse audiences.

For educational reform leaders the Avant-Garde's fearless creativity fuels initiatives that disrupt outdated systems and introduce modern, inclusive practices. Their independent thinking challenges the status quo, ensuring innovative solutions in the public education sector. Or as community engagement specialists for cultural initiatives, the Avant-Garde uses their dynamic style and visionary thinking to bridge diverse cultural groups and foster meaningful dialogue. Their ability to think outside the box ensures programs that are both engaging and impactful.

Avant-Garde personalities shine as Cyber Warfare Strategists in the military where their innovative thinking and unconventional approaches drive creative solutions in ever-evolving digital battlefields. In law enforcement they thrive as Forensic Technology Developers, pushing the boundaries of innovation to create cutting-edge tools that enhance investigative capabilities.

On the flipside, the Avant-Garde may struggle in roles that demand strict adherence to established protocols or that resist change. Positions such as compliance officers or budget analysts that prioritize discipline, consistency, and methodical approaches might stifle their creative spirit. These structured environments may leave them feeling constrained and unable to fully leverage their innovative talents.

The Glamorous: Magnetic and Extravagant

The Glamorous persona is a paragon of attention and fashion, making them a natural fit for leadership in industries such as luxury goods, high-end events, or entertainment public relations.

Their wardrobe is a bastion of opulence, each piece resonating with the allure of a meticulously curated collection. Picture them in attire that captivates with its shimmering details, reflective finishes, and bold color palette, from the fierceness of reds to the solemnity of blacks to the nobility of purples. When it comes to maintaining their wardrobe, they exercise care in trying to preserve each piece as a cherished element of their sumptuous attire. If that doesn't work, no worries, they'll just move on to the next fashion item.

They regard their body as integral to their personal identity; they sculpt their physique to harmonize with their taste and social stature. Their fitness routines are as much a part of their brand narrative as their choice of wardrobe.

Their accessories are selected for their storytelling power and their ability to accentuate their captivating presence. But these pieces don't have to be luxurious jewelry or high-end designer shoes. What matters more than the price tag is how much attention the piece can draw to their look.

Their grooming routines are conducted with the same precision and intentionality as dressing for a gala. Grooming for them is artistry, hair care is a discipline, and skin care is a devotion, each facet executed to radiate charisma and draw admiration. This scrupulous cultivation of their appearance reflects a profound appreciation for its transformative power.

- **Keyword:** attraction
- **Perceived traits:** trendy, stimulating, popular, magnetic, fit, extravagant, daring, attractive, admirable
- **Perceived challenges:** pompous, one-dimensional, manipulative, insincere, indiscreet, flamboyant, deceitful

The Glamorous persona thrives in roles that demand charisma, visibility, and the ability to command attention with presence and style where their magnetic charm and keen eye for presentation enhance public engagement and inspire confidence.

As public-facing community ambassadors, Glamorous leaders shine by fostering relationships between government agencies and the public. Their innate ability to captivate and communicate ensures they are effective in relaying messages and representing their agency in a way that resonates with diverse audiences.

In the role of public affairs specialists, the Glamorous persona's flair for presentation and bold style make them effective in crafting compelling campaigns or engaging with media outlets.

Cultural event coordinators benefit from the Glamorous leader's talent for creating dazzling experiences. Whether planning large-scale public festivals or high-profile ceremonies, their ability to curate memorable moments ensure events that leave lasting impressions. Tourism promotion specialists draw on the Glamorous persona's ability to sell the allure of a destination. Their captivating style and natural enthusiasm make them perfect for highlighting the best aspects of a city, state, or region, encouraging tourism and economic growth.

As political campaign managers the Glamorous persona's flair for spectacle helps energize campaign teams and captivate voters. Their alluring style can support a momentum that drives electoral success.

On the other hand, the Glamorous persona might face difficulties in roles that require subdued, behind-the-scenes work or minimal public interaction. Positions such as data analysts or internal policy researchers, which prioritize quiet diligence and low-profile contributions, might clash with their need for visibility and creative expression. The lack of direct engagement or opportunities to showcase their charisma could leave them feeling unfulfilled.

The Dramatic: Strong and Fearless

The Dramatic persona is an unforgettable presence, embodying a love for the bold and theatrical that can be harnessed in leadership roles from creative directorships to performance arts management.

Their wardrobe is an audacious array of statement pieces that seize attention, mirroring the boldness of their personality. Each piece is a testament to their fearlessness with each item chosen for its impact. It's fashion that doesn't just capture the limelight, it generates it, ensuring they aren't just observed but remembered. Architectural collars, oversized sleeves, and other unconventional silhouettes are their staples, each piece a statement in itself.

They revel in the strength and sophistication of black, black, and more black, allowing it to dominate their wardrobe as the color of their joy. When they opt for other colors they are strategically employed to forge a stark, memorable contrast that complements their daring sartorial narrative.

The maintenance of their wardrobe is as exacting and dramatic as a theater's costume shop: detailed, intentional, and always in pursuit of the remarkable.

They view their body as a stage for a command performance. Their confidence is their most treasured garment, enveloping a physique that is as dynamic as their sartorial choices, making a statement as memorable as their own dramatic essence.

Their accessories and grooming routines are essential to their expressive arsenal. Each piece of jewelry, every selection of shoes, and every grooming choice is a thoughtful act of self-expression, adding bold lines to the story they embody.

For the Dramatic, the world is a vast stage, and they're always in the lead role with each facet of their appearance carefully curated to etch a lasting impression of their indelible presence in any professional setting.

- **Keyword:** power
- **Perceived traits:** strong, intense, charismatic, demanding, bold, commanding, captivating, aloof, severe, spectacular
- **Perceived challenges:** tough, possessive, intrusive, intense, insensitive, harsh, dominating, cold

The Dramatic persona thrives in roles that require bold decision-making, that command attention, and that deliver impactful results.

As public relations strategists, Dramatic leaders excel at crafting narratives that captivate and inspire the public. Their commanding personality ensures that they shine during press conferences, crisis communications, or high-profile events, making them invaluable in shaping the public image of their agency.

As legislative advocates, their intense and charismatic nature allows them to lobby effectively for policy changes. Their ability to communicate passionately and present compelling arguments makes them a force to be reckoned with in legislative chambers and stakeholder meetings.

Civic engagement leaders benefit from the Dramatic persona's captivating presence. Whether organizing rallies or leading community initiatives, their bold approach inspires collective action and empowers constituents to participate in public life. Cultural affairs directors draw on the Dramatic persona's love for the theatrical to curate and promote vibrant arts and cultural programs. Their ability to command attention and engage diverse audiences ensures these initiatives resonate on a grand scale.

Dramatic personalities shine as military drill sergeants where their commanding presence and intense demeanor instill discipline and inspire respect in recruits through powerful demonstrations of authority and precision. In law enforcement they are well-suited as Crisis Management Leaders where their ability to captivate attention and maintain unwavering control is critical in coordinating responses during emergencies and high-pressure situations.

The Dramatic persona might struggle in roles that prioritize diplomacy over dominance or that demand a softer touch. Positions like conflict mediators or ombudspersons, where impartiality and gentle negotiation are key, could be challenging. The Dramatic's intensity and commanding style may come across as too forceful in contexts that require subtlety and restraint.

Did you catch yourself nodding along as you read about one of these secondary personas? Or did you see a bit of yourself in the Caregiver's empathy, the Avant-Garde's creativity, the Glamorous' style, or the Dramatic's flair?

Here's the thing: balance is key. While it's great to tap into these secondary personas when the moment calls for it, leaning too heavily into the extremes can lead to some serious misperceptions.

Take the Caregiver, for instance. Sure, empathy and warmth are crucial for impactful leadership in service and duty, but if they're always showing up in flowing attire with super cute hair and delicate shoes, constantly prioritizing harmony over speaking up, people might start to see them as a one-dimensional nurturer. Their assertiveness and strategic thinking skills, necessary for effective decision-making and crisis management, could be overlooked.

Or how about the Avant-Garde? Their creativity and boundary-pushing nature can be a major asset in policy innovation or public communication, but if they're constantly disrupting meetings with wild ideas, neglecting practicality, and prioritizing bold fashion choices over substance, they risk being pigeonholed as the "out-there" one, overshadowing other valuable qualities.

And although most of us love a bit of shine, if the Glamorous is overdoing it with the hair, makeup, and revealing outfits, people might start to see them as all style, no substance. They might miss the smart, hardworking leader underneath the glitz who's capable of navigating complex governmental structures or public engagements.

Finally, there's the Dramatic. Sure, they can command attention like no other, but if they're always cranking up the intensity, they risk intimidating others and hindering collaboration.

It's all about striking that balance, knowing when to dial up the drama and when to tone it down in the diverse settings.

Again, there's no such thing as a perfect persona. You're uniquely you, and that's what makes you extraordinary. The key is to find harmony between your primary and secondary personas, to let your best self shine through while adapting to different contexts. It's about curating your expression to meet the moment without losing what makes you, well, you.

And should you seek to delve deeper into the fabric of your perceived identity, the end of this book provides a gateway. There you'll find a QR code and a link to a perception persona audit available on my website, a free tool designed to offer insights into which primary or secondary persona you're currently embodying or are perceived as.

Chapter 5
Leaders Look Professional

Strategic Moves to Authority: Positioning for the End Game.

Chapter 5: Leaders Look Professional

Let's time travel back to when professional rules were clearly defined and universally understood, an era when professional identity wasn't just a guideline but a strict code of conduct that almost everyone followed. The rigidity of those rules might seem stifling now, but they also offer a clear road map for how to present yourself in a professional environment. Today, navigating the shifting sands of what defines "professional" in the workplace is an intricate dance. The concept of looking professional for today's leaders is a vibrant tapestry that mirrors the vast expanse of fields related to public service—from government to law enforcement to the military to emergency response—and that reflects diverse cultures, generations, and personal styles. Dress codes used to be the compass that directed the look of leadership. Those sartorial standards were not just about fashion; they were emblems of seriousness, competence, and intent within a professional context. They allowed agencies to create a sense of unity and professionalism through a shared visual standard. But those dress codes have become historical markers from which the present-day's dynamic fashion ethos has emerged. Let's briefly revisit those standards.

Dress code level one: formal attire. Formal attire was once the pinnacle of professional wear. Leaders adorned themselves with classic suits in dark, commanding hues and paired them with pristine white dress shirts. Women maintained standard knee-length skirts or dresses, and accessories were selected for

subtlety—closed-toe dress shoes with pantyhose as an indispensable companion for women, irrespective of the season, and jewelry that whispered of status, such as understated watches or cufflinks. Hair was often styled in a restrained manner, and makeup for women was applied with a light hand to accentuate a look of natural authority.

Dress code level two: professional attire. Professional attire offered a broader palette. Suits branched into lighter colors and subtle patterns, whereas dress shirts could bring a pop of color or a delicate print. Skirts for women relaxed slightly in fit, and footwear expanded to include dress shoes in a variety of colors. Accessories, such as ties or scarves, could introduce a personal touch, and jewelry might make a bolder statement. Hairstyles softened, and makeup for women could venture beyond the bare essentials to enhance confidence and presence.

Dress code level three: business casual. Business casual introduced an even more personal touch to leadership. Blazers paired with slacks or skirts provided a blend of authority and approachability, and fabrics and colors became more diverse. Dress shoes remained the standard, and hair and makeup could echo the wearer's personality, offering a palette for more vivid expression. Accessories allowed more creativity to shine through.

Dress code level four: mainstream casual. Mainstream casual offered a departure from tradition in more relaxed settings. Dress shirts gave way to more relaxed button-downs, even embracing short sleeves for a touch of informality. The color spectrum widened, and patterns became more playful. Footwear could be comfortably chic, reflecting personal style and practicality. Accessories served as a focal point for individuality, and hair could be more freely styled. Makeup for women, in harmony with this casual air, could be more experimental.

Dress code level five: baseline casual. Baseline casual was the embodiment of relaxed professionalism. Denim could be polished enough for a casual work setting, provided it was clean and fit well. Tops could be comfortable yet tasteful, and shoes could range from loafers to well-kept, tasteful sneakers. Hair could be worn in a variety of styles that still conveyed intentionality, and makeup for women could be as understated or as expressive as the overall ensemble allowed. Accessories were chosen for comfort and personal expression.

But now let's pause and consider the present. The rules that once dictated the look of leadership have been blurred by the evolving landscape of the modern workplace, including the public sector. The once rigid frameworks have softened, morphing into a more nuanced spectrum of acceptable workwear for several reasons that we'll examine next.

The concept of "casual" in today's workplace is nebulous and subjective. Ever found yourself staring at your closet, wondering if you could get away with your favorite jeans for a team meeting? While the traditional dress code was meticulously defined, "casual" remains an elusive term, leading to uncertainty. What one person considers business casual might be seen as too informal by another. This ambiguity challenges leaders in service and duty to balance comfort with professionalism. Leaders also must develop a keen sense of appropriateness for various settings, from community events to leadership meetings.

Cultural diversity is reshaping dress norms in the public sector workplace. You might have noticed how meetings today can bring together a vibrant mix of styles, each reflecting different cultural norms. Each culture brings its own perspective on professional identity, adding complexity to the definition of professional or casual dress. What's considered appropriate in one culture might be too formal or too casual in another, particularly in a sector that often serves diverse communities.

Generational views further complicate dress codes. Ever felt a bit out of place because you felt too formal or too relaxed compared to others? Each generation brings its own attitudes toward self-expression and conformity. Older generations might prefer traditional looks, whereas younger generations lean toward more relaxed and individualistic styles. Navigating these generational preferences requires flexibility that honors the values of all generations while maintaining a professional identity.

Agencies emphasizing diversity, equity, and inclusion are reshaping dress codes. Expectations have become way more inclusive in recent years. Recognizing that traditional dress codes can be exclusionary or discriminatory has led to more flexible policies in public service roles, ensuring everyone can express their identities without fear of prejudice or marginalization.

Gender expression is no longer confined to binary norms. Maybe you've seen colleagues who confidently blend traditionally masculine and feminine styles, or perhaps you do this yourself. The binary understanding of gender-specific clothing is giving way to a more fluid perspective. This evolution allows individuals to dress in ways that align with their true selves rather than conforming to outdated norms.

The internet and social media blur fashion lines. Ever bought an outfit you saw on your Instagram feed, only to realize it's probably not appropriate for your role at work? Trends that start online quickly make their way into the workplace, challenging traditional notions of workplace appropriateness.

The pandemic and remote work have fostered informality, reshaping perceptions of professional attire. Remember the pandemic days of video calls that were made while wearing pajamas from the waist down? The shift to remote work introduced a level of informality previously unseen, further blurring the lines, even for roles traditionally performed on-site.

The rise of flexible working arrangements has blurred work-life boundaries, contributing to a more fluid approach to workwear. Have you ever needed an outfit that's as ready for a video call with department heads as it is for a quick site visit to assess infrastructure projects? Service and duty leaders seek to integrate their personal style with their professional identity, requiring versatility and comfort that still presents well across various settings.

Interactions with the public now demand authenticity, leading to a shift away from the traditional "suited and booted" approach to leadership. Have you found your constituents or community leaders respond better when you show a bit more of your personal style? A more relatable look can help build trust and rapport. Leaders now, more than ever, can create a look that reflects their genuine personality and that fosters a sense of connection rather than adhering to outdated standards of professionalism.

Let's face it, the future of workplace style in the public sector is anything but static. It's evolving rapidly, driven by a mix of individualism and changing societal norms. Nevertheless, your professional identity still needs to honor the gravitas of your field while being flexible enough to meet the demands of the modern public service world. Think of it as finding a common visual language that respects the traditions of your profession while embracing the individuality you can now display. Gone are the days of rigid dress codes. The contemporary professional landscape is too dynamic for one-size-fits-all rules. Instead, today's leaders in service and duty need to craft a look of leadership that meets several key functions.

Here's what that look should accomplish:

Bolster your confidence: Your look should make you feel invincible and confident in your skin, ready to tackle any challenge with the poise of a superhero.

Reflect the environment in which you operate: Recognize the sector nuances, the cultural ethos of your agency or institution, or the expectations tied to your role, whether you're addressing senior leaders in government or representing your team at a community initiative.

Consider the audience you will encounter: Don't dress just for the position you hold but for the individuals you serve and collaborate with, from elected officials to diverse community leaders.

Facilitate versatility: It's about selecting pieces that can be mixed and matched to suit any engagement or unexpected encounters you might have throughout the day.

Demonstrate deliberate choices: Show that your style is a thoughtful and intentional component of your professional tool kit.

Pay attention to details: Recognize that grooming, accessories, or the right finishing touches are the final steps to an intentional look that speaks to your attention to detail.

Invest in quality over quantity: If you show that you invest in yourself, others assume you have the capability to invest in them too, reflecting the high standards of public service.

Balance current trends with classic staples: Ensure your wardrobe remains relevant yet timeless.

Know the narrative you want to express: With each piece reflecting a chapter of your personal identity, align your external presentation with your internal values and the mission of your agency or institution.

Complement rather than overshadow your intrinsic talents and abilities: Use pieces to accentuate your look of leadership without causing unnecessary distraction from your expertise.

Allow your presence to take center stage: Adopt a look that doesn't clamor for attention but supports your professional identity in delivering impactful and meaningful service.

Avoid the pitfall of feeling compelled to mirror traditionally gendered dress expectations: Assert that competence and authority in public service are not monopolized by any gender identity.

Eschew the pressure to conform to gender norms: Reinforce the idea that your value is not predicated on these norms but on your expertise and contributions to the public sector.

Embrace trial and error as part of the refinement process: Experiment with new looks and evolve your look of leadership based on feedback and self-reflection.

Lastly, let's rethink a familiar saying, one you might have heard or even shared yourself: "Dress for the job you want, not the one you have." While there's truth in that, let's broaden our view. Instead of just aiming for the next step, consider your ultimate career goal.

Envision the pinnacle of your public service career. Perhaps it's to become the head of a key government agency, a transformative community leader, or a policy innovator at the forefront of social change. Or maybe it's becoming a renowned advocate for public welfare, an expert in disaster response, or a top adviser in national security.

Whatever your goal, it's vital to begin embodying that role as early as possible to give yourself and others the chance to see the potential in you right now.

Your wardrobe should be a reflection of your ambition and a projection of your potential, the zenith of your aspirations. Hence, each day is an opportunity to illustrate not just where you are or where you want to be next, but where you're ultimately determined to be.

Prescribed Uniformity in Action

Ever noticed how uniforms speak volumes without uttering a word? When we encounter a concierge in their distinctive attire, it can evoke feelings of trust and expectations of expert local knowledge. A chef's whites instantly convey the weight of culinary expertise and food safety standards. Similarly, the tailored scrubs of a veterinarian signal care and professionalism for your beloved pets, while the sharp uniforms of airline pilots and cabin crew instill confidence and calm during your travels. In creative fields such as stage productions, the costumes of theater performers embody the characters and stories they bring to life. Uniforms are omnipresent, offering a visual shorthand that connects the role, the individual, and the expectations of those they serve.

And, of course, in many public sector professions, uniforms are silent ambassadors too, instantly recognizable symbols that communicate volumes. A uniform serves as a bridge between the role, the person wearing the uniform, and those they serve.

Take law enforcement officers, for example. When you see professionals adorned with badges, tactical gear, or dress uniforms, you immediately recognize them as figures of authority and public safety. Their uniform is a bastion of professionalism, instantly commanding respect and projecting the power vested in their roles as guardians of order and justice.

Or consider firefighters and paramedics. Their distinct uniforms do more than just signify their roles; they represent immediate action, preparedness, and a commitment to life-saving service. The reflective stripes, functional gear, and unmistakable helmets are emblems of their dedication and readiness to respond to emergencies with courage and skill. In the military, uniforms are steeped in tradition and significance. Each insignia, medal, or patch tells a story of rank, expertise, and service. Military attire is not merely functional; it is a symbol of discipline, loyalty, and sacrifice. From dress uniforms at ceremonial events to combat gear in the field, the uniform communicates the wearer's role, experience, and unwavering dedication to their nation.

In judicial and correctional services the uniform carries dual meanings of authority and accountability. Correctional officers, for instance, wear uniforms that denote their responsibility to maintain order and security within challenging environments while court officers signal their critical roles in legal proceedings.

Uniforms carry a profound psychological weight, serving as silent ambassadors of authority, trust, and professionalism. Beyond authority, uniforms also create a powerful sense of unity and shared identity. By visually aligning team members, uniforms foster camaraderie and morale, bridging hierarchical gaps by emphasizing collective purpose over individual differences. For example, in emergency response teams or military units the uniform symbolizes the shared mission and mutual reliance among team members. This sense of belonging not only enhances internal cohesion but also reinforces public perception of an organized, disciplined, and collaborative entity. When worn with pride and maintained meticulously, uniforms are far more than just garments, they are the embodiment of professionalism and solidarity.

In moments of crisis, uniforms are more than functional attire. They become beacons of reassurance. A firefighter's uniform at a disaster site instantly communicates help, safety, and order. Visual cues such as insignia, logos, and color schemes provide critical information about roles and expertise, allowing the public to quickly identify who is in charge and where to seek assistance. This immediate recognition is vital in chaotic situations where clarity and direction can save lives. Uniforms symbolize the reliability and readiness of the wearer, calming those in distress by signaling that capable hands are at work.

For the professionals wearing them, uniforms also reinforce their sense of purpose and authority, allowing them to step into their roles with confidence. In these moments a uniform becomes a visual anchor for trust and stability, embodying the professionalism and commitment that is essential in critical scenarios.

I could go on and on. Uniforms are omnipresent and crucial in the public sector. They play a significant role across a vast array of public service professions.

But the way the public perceives uniforms profoundly shapes interactions between professionals and the communities they serve. A law enforcement uniform may evoke feelings of safety and order for some, but others might view it through a lens of skepticism based on personal or societal experiences. Similarly, a paramedic's uniform can bring immediate comfort and hope, signaling help and care during vulnerable moments, yet it might also evoke feelings of distress or fear if associated with traumatic events or critical emergencies. A firefighter's uniform, often seen as a symbol of heroism, also might stir anxiety in individuals who have experienced devastating fires or evacuations. Likewise, the formal attire of a judge, intended to represent fairness and justice, could be perceived as intimidating or alienating by those who feel marginalized by the judicial system. These varied perceptions highlight the complex interplay between uniforms and the emotional context of those who encounter them.

These perceptions underscore the importance of not only maintaining a professional appearance but also of embodying the values the uniform represents. By aligning their actions with the ideals their uniform symbolizes, professionals can build trust and strengthen their connection with the public they serve. Because the relationship between a uniform and the professional wearing it is both intimate and public, it can kindle a sense of belonging and purpose, creating an instant visual connection with the community.

It's important that you emphasize these principles and help your team understand how crucial it is to wear their uniform with pride, professionalism, and attention to detail. It's not just a garment; it's a messenger that allows them to convey their commitment to service excellence and public sector values.

Nevertheless, sometimes they might feel restricted by wearing a uniform, perceiving it as a limitation on their personal choices or an obstacle to expressing their individual style. But such a perspective overlooks the opportunity uniforms provide to enhance their professional identity.

A uniform doesn't erase individuality. Instead, it serves as a foundation upon which personal touches and distinctive elements can shine, all within the framework of professionalism. Through thoughtful grooming, accessories, and even posture, team members can still reflect their unique personalities while embodying the brand's values.

Sometimes the choice of accessories, even within professional boundaries, can make subtle yet impactful distinctions. Where regulations permit, the flair of a tasteful pin or the understated elegance of a classic watch can highlight personal style without straying from the required uniformity. A patterned tie or a functional yet stylish belt can serve as a unique identifier, and a slight variation in footwear or the style or color of socks can add a discreet touch of personality. Hair accessories used to secure styles can be both practical and a reflection of individual taste.

The meticulous care of a uniform—the sharpness of a crease, the precision of a tuck, the cleanliness and crispness of the fabric—can convey dedication to the role and attention to detail. These choices, although seemingly minor, can significantly impact how team members are perceived and, more important, how they perceive themselves within their roles. It's in these meticulously maintained details that individual pride and professionalism shine.

The management of uniform policies often presents a tapestry of challenges, each thread representing a unique perspective or attitude among team members. While uniforms serve as the public sector's silent ambassadors, the individuals wearing them bring a spectrum of responses that require astute handling. Let us delve into the various types of team reactions to uniforms.

The Complacent Conformist: Some team members embrace uniforms as a reprieve from the daily sartorial decision-making process. While their acceptance is welcome, it can breed complacency. These team members may not fully grasp the power of a well-maintained uniform in elevating public perception and fostering trust. Their attitude, though seemingly positive, can lead to a lackadaisical approach to uniform care and presentation,

potentially undermining the authority or professionalism associated with their role. A postal worker neglecting to wear their official badge or uniform jacket, for instance, might unintentionally signal disorganization, diminishing the public's trust in their service.

The Rule-Bending Individualist: At the opposite end of the spectrum are those team members who view uniforms as constraints on their personal expression. These team members might subtly (or not so subtly) push boundaries, seeking ways to infuse their individuality into their mandated attire. Their creativity, while admirable, can challenge the consistency and professionalism that uniforms are designed to convey, particularly in roles like law enforcement or emergency response where uniformity is critical to public trust and perception. Take a park ranger who adds a brightly colored scarf or nonregulation hat to their uniform. It may draw attention, but it detracts from the cohesive image their role requires.

The Inconsistent Adopter: Some team members oscillate between compliance and negligence, presenting a challenge of inconsistency. Their adherence to uniform standards may wax and wane based on factors like mood, schedule, or perceived importance of their assignment. This unpredictability can create confusion among the public and frustration among leadership, undermining the uniform's role in projecting authority and reliability. An example of this might be a corrections officer who meticulously follows uniform standards during inspections but neglects them during routine duties, unintentionally signaling a lack of commitment.

The Comfort Seeker: Certain team members prioritize comfort over presentation, potentially compromising the polished image required in public-facing roles. These individuals may alter their uniforms in ways that enhance personal comfort but detract from their professional appearance. While a desire for comfort is understandable, it can conflict with the uniform's purpose of projecting a professional and prepared image. Picture a firefighter opting for more comfortable, nonregulation footwear. While understandable, such a choice dilutes the professional identity the uniform is designed to project.

The Detail Dismisser: These team members may wear the uniform but overlook crucial details—a missing badge, scuffed boots, or wrinkled shirts—that detract from the overall professional identity. While they may argue that details don't matter, these seemingly minor oversights can significantly impact public perceptions and erode trust, especially in roles where attention to detail symbolizes competence. Imagine a law enforcement officer with an improperly aligned insignia or an unpolished badge, potentially undermining the authority their uniform is meant to convey.

The Cultural Considerate: Some team members may have cultural or religious practices that conflict with standard uniform policies. While these requests are rooted in deeply held values and deserve respect, they can present challenges for agencies striving to maintain consistency and cohesion in their uniform policies. Striking a balance between inclusivity and uniformity can be a complex endeavor that requires thoughtful consideration and, at times, compromises that may not fully satisfy all parties. For example, a request from a team member to wear religiously mandated robes that significantly deviate from the uniform's design and functional requirements—such as a firefighter's protective gear—may highlight the inherent limitations of accommodating certain practices without compromising operational safety or consistency.

The Gender Equality Advocate: These team members are sensitive to gender biases in uniform design, such as impractical or overly gendered uniforms. They may voice concerns about comfort, functionality, or the message conveyed by traditional uniform choices. For instance, they might question whether uniforms for female firefighters or police officers are designed with practicality and equality in mind. Their perspective challenges agencies to rethink traditional uniform designs and adopt more inclusive,

equitable approaches. Consider a female police officer advocating for tailored designs that ensure functionality during high-pressure situations, pushing against outdated uniform norms.

The Sustainability Champion: With growing environmental awareness, some team members may express concerns about the ecological impact of uniform production and disposal. These individuals often advocate for more sustainable fabric choices, ethical manufacturing processes, and responsible practices for uniform disposal. Their passion for sustainability can drive positive changes in uniform policies, such as introducing recycled materials or extending uniform lifespans, but changes also may conflict with budgetary or practical considerations in public sector procurement. One example could be a military officer championing uniforms made from sustainable, durable materials that align with environmental goals while meeting operational demands.

The Body Positive Advocate: These team members may struggle with uniform policies that don't accommodate diverse body types or physical needs. They often push for a wider range of sizes, more inclusive designs, and adaptable uniform options. Their advocacy highlights the importance of ensuring that all team members feel comfortable and confident in their work attire, regardless of body shape or physical requirements. Picture a corrections officer requiring tailored uniforms to ensure mobility, demonstrating the importance of comfort and inclusivity in such a demanding role.

The Uniform Upseller: Some team members excel in uniform compliance and understand its value in public interactions. These team members can be powerful allies in promoting a culture of uniform excellence. They often take pride in their appearance and may even suggest improvements to uniform designs or policies. Their positive attitude toward uniforms can be contagious, influencing other team members and enhancing the overall professional identity of their team or agency. Think of a picture-

perfect customs officer who keeps their uniform meticulously clean and pressed, setting a standard of professionalism that inspires their colleagues.

If you found yourself nodding along or thinking, *Yes, I have one of these on my team*, to more than one of these types, you're not alone. And therein lies the crux of the matter: no general dress code or uniform rulebook can address all these issues comprehensively. The source or reason behind each team member's attitude toward uniforms might be as unique as the individual themselves. Instead of relying solely on blanket policies, you need to adopt a more nuanced approach. Effective uniform management requires a combination of clear guidelines, open communication, and individualized strategies. By taking the time to understand the underlying motivations and concerns of your team members, you can craft solutions that not only ensure compliance but also foster a sense of pride and ownership in wearing the uniform.

Remember, your goal isn't to enforce rules but to cultivate an environment where the uniform is respected as an integral part of the professional identity of both the individual and the agency. By leading with intention and understanding, you can transform the concept of uniformity from a mere policy requirement into a powerful tool for building trust, fostering pride, and showcasing the values your team and agency stand for.

Silent Standards and Unwritten Uniforms

You might find yourself in a position of leadership that doesn't require you to wear the same uniform as your team, or perhaps you've chosen a career path in the public sector that commonly doesn't mandate formal uniforms. You might be a city planner where your role involves navigating between community forums and high-level strategy meetings. Or perhaps you're a policy advisor working in government offices where your attire needs to reflect both professionalism and accessibility.

In these roles you might think, *I'm free from any restrictions and uniforms.* If so, it's time to think again. Every field in the public sector, every agency, and every role operates within a set of unspoken expectations—silent standards that make up the unwritten uniform for you as a leader in service and duty. These unwritten standards exist in the collective consciousness of your field.

Think about high-profile government offices. Even without a formal mandate, the unspoken uniform often includes conservative suits, crisp shirts, and understated accessories for leadership roles. Consider local government outreach programs where the emphasis might be on practical, approachable attire that fosters community trust. In creative fields within public service, like cultural event planning or civic arts programs, the expectation may lean toward eclectic attire that reflects innovation and forward-thinking approaches. On the other hand, leaders in high-stakes departments such as public health or emergency management often default to polished, no-nonsense outfits that project authority and preparedness. The unifying thread is that each unspoken uniform aims to visually personify professional archetypes and establish a tribal signaling system that everyone can subconsciously read at a glance.

By decoding these silent standards you can navigate your role in the public sector with a more nuanced understanding of these unarticulated yet powerful norms. It's about reading the room, understanding the culture, and dressing in a way that communicates you belong, that you're a credible player in the field, and that you respect the unspoken rules of the game. So how do you decode what your silent uniform should look like in your role?

Start with a simple observation. Look around your workplace or domain in the public sector or government service. Is there a common thread in how leaders dress? You're not aiming to copy anyone but rather to understand the visual language and subtle cues leaders offer. Notice the colors, fits, patterns, and levels of formality. Pay attention to the details: the type of watches, shoes, the hairstyles, or the makeup. These subtleties are your road map.

Consider the context of your interactions. When you're in senior leadership meetings, what's the dominant style? At community events, which styles seem to exude success and influence? These observations act as your guideposts. From community forums to casual Fridays, each setting has its unwritten rules that, once cracked, can be a powerful tool in your arsenal.

Reflect on your role within the agency or department. What are the expectations—both spoken and unspoken—for someone in your position? How can your look of leadership showcase your professional identity without saying a word?

Then think about how far you can integrate your personal touch. Once you grasp the silent standards of your field in the public sector, you can subtly bend them. It's important to find a balance between sector expectations and your personal style—the sweet spot where your silent uniform empowers you to feel authentic and confident in your professional skin. Remember, your silent uniform isn't just about fitting in; it's about standing out in the right ways. It's about aligning your external presentation with your career aspirations and the persona you want to project.

Let's circle back to our earlier discussion on perception personas where we highlighted the power of keywords for each of the seven personas—comfort, values, quality, care, creativity, attraction, and power—that anchor our professional identities. You might find that your unwritten uniform speaks to these keywords and the perceived traits they represent in your role.

It might explain why you feel seamlessly integrated in some settings but like a fish out of water in others. This is not about changing your professional identity. It's about fine-tuning by focusing on the following factors:

- **Balancing personas:** Everyone has a primary persona and one or more secondary personas. It's about leveraging this spectrum appropriately. For example, your Caregiver qualities may be front and center in a community engagement role, whereas your secondary Avant-Garde traits can shine when innovating public awareness campaigns or initiatives. Balancing personas is about the strategic interplay between different facets. It recognizes that a leader in service and duty isn't one-dimensional—you can be nurturing and innovative, methodical and creative, caring and authoritative all at once. By emphasizing certain traits in specific contexts, you can align your professional identity with your role's expectations while maintaining your unique essence. This alignment allows you to connect with others on multiple levels and in various scenarios.

- **Borrowing elements:** This factor involves selectively adopting characteristics from other personas when needed. A Glamorous persona might borrow elements from the Cosmopolitan's flair for quality when attending a high-profile government event, or a Traditionalist could incorporate the Caregiver's warmth for a community-focused retreat or event. Borrowing elements means curating aspects from other personas to complement your dominant traits. This selective synthesis creates a dynamic professional identity that can adapt and thrive across different settings. It's about enriching your personal narrative by integrating diverse qualities that broaden your appeal and enhance your influence. This nuanced approach allows you to be perceived as multifaceted and versatile, showcasing your ability to evolve and respond to various professional challenges.

Frankly, you also can choose to disrupt these patterns of unspoken uniforms. History is full of leaders who have shattered expectations and redefined governmental or public sector norms, becoming icons of success with their unique looks.

Yet, it's essential to recognize that these cases are rare. They stand out against a backdrop of more typical narratives. For every convention-defying success story there are countless others who navigate the intricate dance of expectations and self-expression with more subtlety. The most common pathway to success in the public sector often involves aligning with established norms while finding small but significant ways to showcase individuality.

Ultimately, the decision is deeply personal. Your career, your professional identity, your style—these are yours to define. And this isn't about surrendering to the status quo; it's about making informed choices, because the silent uniform of your sector or role doesn't need to be a straitjacket; it can be a canvas—sometimes for blending in, sometimes for standing out. The art is in knowing when to do which, and the wisdom is in recognizing that the choice is always, unequivocally, yours.

Internal Mandates We Self-Enforce

Yes, you read that right. Many of us are guilty of setting unwritten rules for ourselves, internal guidelines we adhere to—often unconsciously—that shape our professional identity. These self-imposed standards can be as binding as uniform policies or official dress codes, yet they stem not from agency mandates but from our own insecurities and the societal expectations we've absorbed over time.

This self-enforcement can manifest in numerous ways, subtly dictating our choices. These are the mental garments made up of beliefs about how we need to appear to be accepted, respected, and successful in our role.

It's time to take a closer look at the expectations some of us have built for ourselves, so let's unfold a few of them.

Conforming to traditionally masculine dress codes is deeply rooted in the historical context of the workplace, especially in fields like law enforcement, the military, and public administration where traditionally masculine attire has long been associated with authority and leadership. It's not uncommon for thoughts like these to cross women's minds: *Should I dress more like my male counterparts to be taken seriously as a senior leader in government? Will I be seen as less authoritative if I don't adopt a masculine style?* Such thoughts are understandable given the long-standing association between masculine attire and power in leadership. But this approach is outdated and not recommended.

First, such an approach can suppress your unique identity, compelling you to fit into an aesthetic that may not resonate with your personal style or the full breadth of your professional capabilities. If traditionally masculine attire feels inauthentic to you, it can affect your confidence and performance in critical interactions whether in the courtroom, on the podium, or in front of your team.

Second, this notion might unintentionally uphold the very gender biases many sectors are striving to overcome. It implies that, to be a leader, you must downplay attributes that aren't traditionally masculine (or feminine).

Instead, choose a look that reflects your professional identity and personal style that allows a richer expression of leadership. This isn't about clothes overshadowing capability; rather, it's about reinforcing that authority and professionalism are defined by your actions and knowledge, not the cut or color of your clothing.

Dressing in an overly gendered manner to emphasize gender identity can be a nuanced issue as well. For some women, this might manifest as a tendency to overdo it—the boldest lipstick, the most dramatic eye makeup, the perfectly coiffed hair, the form-fitting outfit, or an excessive use of accessories. In the pursuit of emphasizing their femininity they may lean toward an overly glamorized appearance that can detract from their professional credibility.

In contrast, some men might fall into the trap of believing that paying attention to their appearance is somehow unmasculine. They may shun any form of grooming or avoid anything that could be perceived as "styling." In an attempt to appear more masculine, they may neglect basic self-care, like keeping uniforms properly pressed or maintaining a neat appearance in public-facing roles.

Just as adopting a predominantly masculine wardrobe can have pitfalls for women (and vice versa), so too can an excessively gendered presentation. It risks diverting attention from your competence to your appearance, overshadowing your professional expertise with personal aesthetics. The silent but potent subtext is that your professional value is intertwined with conventional beauty standards or gender stereotypes, potentially undermining the respect you command based on merit and accomplishments.

Although there's power in embracing and expressing your gender identity, it's crucial to find a balance that doesn't tip into excess. The key is striking a harmonious chord between asserting your gender identity and underscoring your professional identity.

Prioritizing others' needs over your own often goes hand in hand with minimizing attention to yourself or personal expenses. You might think, *I shouldn't spend too much on my wardrobe when my family needs resources,* or *It's selfish to focus on my appearance when there are more important things to worry about.* You may find yourself allocating resources—time, money, and energy—to support and uplift others, even if it means your needs take a backseat. But doing so can result in a professional identity, including your wardrobe, that doesn't reflect your status or ambition but that does affect how you're perceived. There's a fine line between being resourceful and neglecting or underselling yourself. Consistently limiting expenditures on yourself might unwittingly signal that you don't value yourself or your role as much as you should. Managing your finances is wise, but it's also important to recognize that investing in your professional identity is not mere vanity, it's an integral part of your positioning.

The goal is to achieve a balance where caring for others doesn't come at the expense of neglecting your own needs. Recognize that you can be a supportive leader while still honoring your personal and professional requirements. Allow yourself permission to invest in your professional identity to feel confident and capable, reflecting the leader in service and duty that you are.

Holding on to the belief that what has worked for years will continue to serve you well can be another pitfall. Perhaps you've caught yourself thinking, *I've always dressed this way, and it's worked, so why change now?* as you glance proudly at a twenty-year-old suit hanging in your wardrobe. But others might perceive an unchanging appearance as a reluctance to adapt to new career phases or interpret it as a lack of investment in your professional growth. In the public sector, where visual cues often communicate ambition and commitment, an unaltered look could signal complacency or resistance to change. This isn't about chasing every fleeting trend or dismissing the value of timeless statement pieces, but when years turn into a decade with the same look, it may be time to acknowledge that your choices are speaking volumes. Periodically updating your professional attire signals that you're evolving, attuned to the present, and invested in your career journey. Updating your look of leadership isn't frivolity, it's a strategic refresh that signals your continued evolution in your public service career and beyond.

Struggling with an "age-appropriate" look is a tug-of-war that spans the spectrum of leaders' careers. You may have caught yourself wondering, *Am I dressing too young for my age as a senior public administrator?* or *Should I dress more conservatively to be taken seriously in my government role?* As a leader in service and duty you might wrestle with the expectation of dressing in a way that aligns with perceived age norms—being trendy and youthful or reserved and mature. This self-imposed standard can be confining, often leading to a look that feels out of sync with your personal identity.

The challenge lies in transcending these societal dictates that attempt to define what is suitable for various ages. Such constraints can dilute your individuality and inadvertently send messages about your capability or currency in the workplace that are misaligned with your actual attributes and contributions. In crafting your professional identity, the aim should not be to camouflage your age but to celebrate the individual you are at every stage of your journey. Acknowledging that every wrinkle has been earned and every fresh perspective is valuable can resonate more deeply than any attempt to conform to narrow age expectations.

Feeling the need to dress down or appear less successful to avoid intimidating or alienating others is a notion that can inadvertently undermine your authority as a leader in service and duty. Thoughts like *If I dress too well, will my team think I'm out of touch?* or *Should I dress more casually to seem more relatable to constituents?* might have crossed your mind. This mentality stems from an attempt to foster relatability, but it risks devaluing your professional expertise. Although approachability is admirable, compromising your professional identity can backfire. Others may subconsciously interpret an overly casual appearance as a lack of engagement or investment in them. It signals that you aren't representing the importance of the services you provide to the public. You want others to feel respected and understood, not condescended to. The key is finding the balance of projecting success in your role without appearing unapproachable or out of touch.

Minimizing efforts under the assumption that skills, not appearance, are what matter is an understandable perspective for many leaders. Perhaps you've thought, *My work for the community should speak for itself. I don't need to put effort into my appearance*, or *I'm too busy focusing on departmental operations to worry about how I look.* The intention of prioritizing substance over superficial style is admirable, but especially in leadership roles, putting minimal effort into your visual presence can unintentionally signal complacency about your professional identity.

While certainly not the prime factor, your self-presentation directly impacts how your leadership abilities are perceived, fair or not. Potential doubts can creep in about commitment and respect for the role when you appear disheveled. The reality is that top performance in leadership requires multifaceted efforts, including conscientious self-presentation. It's about projecting pride in yourself and the responsibilities of representing an agency with gravitas.

Limiting self-expression in professional settings is a self-limiting belief often rooted in deep-seated cultural, familial, and societal norms. Perhaps you've told yourself, *I shouldn't stand out too much at work in this traditional agency,* or *This never was appropriate at work, so why now?* This learned behavior, ingrained from an early age, can become a barrier to showcasing the full richness of your professional identity. Authentic self-expression through clothing is a form of nonverbal communication that speaks volumes about your confidence, creativity, and leadership style. It's about striking a balance between respecting workplace decorum and embracing the distinctive qualities that set you apart in your role. By gently pushing against these inherited boundaries of self-expression you open the door to a wardrobe that's not just acceptable but also memorable and true to who you are. It's about allowing yourself to shine within the framework of your professional environment, contributing your unique style to the chorus in a way that is harmoniously yours.

Assuming the "perfection" burden is a self-imposed standard in which you believe every aspect of your appearance must be flawless. Perhaps you've found yourself obsessing over every detail of your appearance before addressing a press conference or leading a team briefing. Rooted in the idea that respect and competence are tied to a faultless image, this belief places immense pressure on you to maintain an impeccable facade at all times. This burden is not just about appearing professional; it's deeply intertwined with the fear of judgment and the desire for acceptance, leading to heightened anxiety and a critical self-view.

But perfection is unattainable, and pursuing it obscures the truth that authenticity and relatability are more compelling than flawlessness. The most respected leaders in service and duty present themselves as human and capable of embracing their imperfections. Releasing yourself from the perfection burden doesn't mean abandoning self-care or professionalism; it means redefining what those concepts mean to you in your role. It's about accepting minor imperfections and recognizing that your value as a leader is not solely contingent on an immaculate appearance.

These self-imposed standards, these "shadow uniforms" are only a few of the barriers we might unconsciously build around ourselves. So now let's take a moment to reframe this discussion. Imagine if, instead of being restricted by these invisible rules, you could harness them as a source of strength and clarity. What if, instead of confining your professional identity, you allowed it to evolve, embracing the full spectrum of who you are? It's about breaking free from the self-imposed limitations that may have held you back, recognizing the power you hold to redefine what your professional identity looks like on your own terms. How much more impactful could you be if you fully embraced your professional identity in every interaction? What new heights could your career reach if you stopped adhering to outdated norms and, instead, set your own standards, driven by confidence and clarity?

Dressing beyond the Code: Situational Awareness

Picture yourself in the eye of a tornado, a place of eerie calm amidst the chaos swirling around you where you might feel a sense of stability and a confidence in your own identity. But step outside that center, and you're instantly swept up in a maelstrom of changing contexts, shifting expectations, and unpredictable situations. For your professional identity, understanding the nuances of each context is like reading the wind patterns of a tornado. It allows you to navigate spaces with the acumen your role demands, adapting your look of leadership accordingly.

This situational awareness communicates your agility and recognition of the subtleties of each situation, ensuring your visual presence contributes positively to the narrative of your leadership. Just as a tornado's intensity can vary, there will be times when the usual rules of appearance won't apply, and a different approach will be needed.

It's also important to acknowledge that many leaders in the service and duty sector operate within the confines of prescribed uniforms where such adaptations aren't available. For these leaders, situational awareness shifts from personal wardrobe adjustments to ensuring that the uniform itself is worn with the appropriate symbolism and care for the context. Thus, the following applies primarily to those leaders not bound by uniform requirements. At times such leaders will need to do the following:

Consider times of crisis or significant institutional change when leaders may forgo traditional formal attire for something that reflects solidarity with their teams and adaptability. In such scenarios it's less about form and more about symbolism. Think of a community crisis, a significant restructuring in an agency, a large-scale emergency response, or sector-wide challenges facing public services. In such instances, choosing a look that is practical, durable, and less formal is crucial. These choices, intentional and considerate, signal that you're fully engaged with and empathetic to the challenges at hand. It's about rolling up your sleeves, both metaphorically and literally, to lead with empathy and readiness, emphasizing that leadership isn't just about directing from above but about being with your team in the trenches of public service.

Now imagine the opposite: A leader overseeing disaster relief efforts shows up at a flood-affected site in an immaculate suit and polished shoes, completely out of sync with the realities on the ground. Not only does this choice highlight their lack of practicality, but it also sends a tone-deaf message to their team and the community that they are disconnected from the urgency and gravity of the situation. Such a misstep could erode trust, making the leader seem out of touch and undermining their credibility.

On the other hand, picture a public health official during a vaccination drive at a community center. They arrive dressed in comfortable, weather-appropriate clothing that aligns with the outdoor setting, and they're wearing a simple but recognizable agency badge. Their approachable demeanor and practical attire demonstrate an understanding of the situation and a commitment to being present when it matters most. This thoughtful alignment reinforces confidence in their leadership and inspires both the team and the public they serve.

Accept that practicality can beat professionalism or personal style. In the diverse environments that define public sector work, practical considerations often have to influence your look of leadership. For example, a leader visiting disaster recovery sites might prioritize rugged and weather-appropriate attire over their usual formal wear to demonstrate preparedness and solidarity. Similarly, if you're a leader in public health or infrastructure, when you step out from your administrative office to visit field operations you may need to adapt your look of leadership, not just to ensure safety and practicality, but also to show that you understand the circumstances and environments in which your team members work. In these situations your appearance of leadership is not only about looking the part but about facilitating the part.

Consider the consequences of an emergency response leader arriving at the site of a wildfire dressed in an elegant suit and dress shoes. Their attire not only limits their ability to move safely but also signals a lack of preparedness and disconnect from the urgency of the situation. This oversight can inadvertently alienate their team and diminish the morale of those looking to them for guidance. Contrast this with a city official overseeing a major infrastructure repair project after a natural disaster. By wearing sturdy boots, high-visibility safety gear, and practical clothing suitable for the environment, they demonstrate a readiness to engage directly with both the team on the ground and the pressing challenges at hand. This choice underscores their commitment to the task and fosters respect from the team and the community alike.

Understand you're a leader at all times, not just during work hours. Your omnipresent professional identity means that perception is continuous, and the silent dialogue of your look of leadership is always engaged. You need to remember you are a visible symbol of someone in a position of influence in your agency 24/7/365. Even in the absence of your team members, colleagues, or senior leaders, your look of leadership should always subtly communicate your role. This means, from the coffee shop to the plane where a random encounter with a potential community partner or government official could occur, your wardrobe choices should always bridge the gap between personal downtime and professional readiness.

Picture a senior public health official spotted at a local grocery store in disheveled clothing during a high-profile health crisis. The contrast between their public-facing role as a trusted authority and their casual, unkempt appearance in a public setting could undermine confidence in their leadership, especially when the community expects visible reassurance and composure. This moment, though unintentional, might cast doubt on their ability to handle the crisis effectively. On the other hand, imagine a state official returning from a weekend hike who stops at a coffee shop in clean, well-kept casual wear such as tailored jeans and a neatly pressed, button-down shirt. Though off duty, their appearance conveys a balance of approachability and professionalism. When a community member recognizes them and strikes up a conversation, the official's readiness to engage while maintaining a polished appearance reinforces trust and admiration, leaving a positive impression that aligns with their leadership role.

Guide your team in understanding this concept. Encourage team members to consider their visual presence as an extension of their professional identity, no matter the setting. Foster an understanding that there's always a level of consideration in how each team member reflects the shared identity of your agency or institution. Your leadership in this aspect sets the tone, signaling to your team that professional identity is a constant that is

ingrained in the very fabric of who you are as a public service collective. By guiding your team in these nuances, you reinforce the trust and reputation of your agency, strengthening public confidence in both leaders and the agency you represent.

Consider a team leader who neglects to address a team member's repeated lapses in uniform adherence during public-facing events. Over time this inconsistency creates an environment in which others feel less inclined to maintain the standards of professionalism. The resulting disarray projects an image of disorganization to the public, diminishing the agency's credibility and eroding the collective morale of the team. In contrast, envision a leader in service and duty who conducts a thoughtful workshop with their team about the importance of appearance in shaping public trust. They highlight the ways in which polished uniforms or cohesive attire reflect the agency's values and commitment to service. By leading with clarity and empathy they cultivate a sense of pride and ownership among their team, ensuring that every member understands their role in maintaining a unified and professional identity, even under challenging circumstances.

In the midst of the swirling winds of modern leadership in service and duty, situational awareness has emerged as a key navigational tool. But it's more than just a tool; it's a mindset, a way of being that separates the leaders who merely survive from those who thrive. By adapting your look to each unique context, you're not just reacting to change; you're driving it. You're showing that leadership in public service isn't about maintaining the status quo but about embracing what's needed, here and now.

In the end, your look of leadership is about so much more than clothing or appearance. It's about embodying the essence of who you are and what you stand for. It's about harnessing the power of your presence to inspire, to innovate, and to lead with unshakable conviction. That's what sets the leaders apart from the followers: the skill to read any room or situation and the courage to be an adaptable guide in any storm that might appear in the ever-changing public service landscape.

Chapter 6
Leaders Look Respectful

Failing to Respect Yourself Casts Doubt on Your Ability to Respect Others.

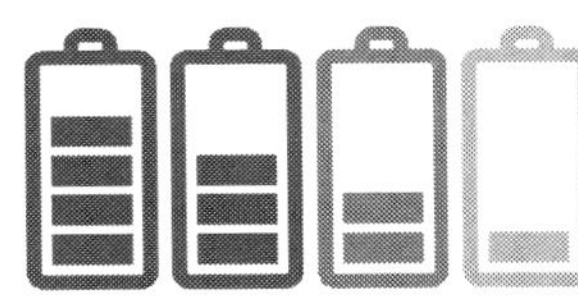

Chapter 6: Leaders Look Respectful

Envision a boomerang gliding through the air and carving a smooth, curved path against the clear sky. As it travels it spins with a perfect balance and rhythm. At the pinnacle of its journey, it pauses momentarily before starting its return. With steady precision, it heads back to the hand that launched it, drawn by an invisible force—most of the time. This is the essence of respect in leadership. The respect you give—to yourself, your team, your community, and your agency—is the force that propels your leadership journey forward. And, like a boomerang, the respect you give will most likely come back to you, shaping the trajectory of your career and the impact you have in the public sector. But respect in leadership is not a single, simple thing. It's a multifaceted gem, each facet reflecting a different aspect of your professional identity—the way you carry yourself, the way you communicate, and the way you make decisions. And, of course, it's also reflected in the way you present yourself.

A respectful professional identity starts with self-respect. When you show respect to yourself through your visual presence, you feel more confident and capable as a leader in service and duty. This confidence translates into your actions, decision-making, and overall demeanor in public interactions and team management. Your respectful presence becomes a silent ambassador, a visible manifestation of self-regard, and a sophisticated acknowledgment of the tremendous responsibility you carry as a leader in service and duty.

Your respectful professional identity sets the tone for your team. Your respectful presence conveys an unspoken commitment to conducting business at the highest professional standards, ensuring serious matters are handled with the necessary gravitas and discernment in public service operations. When team members see you consistently presenting yourself with respect, they're more likely to follow your lead and embody the same standards you do.

For constituents, your respectful professional identity is a testament to your dedication and reliability. It articulates values and sets a tone for interactions, signaling that you're a serious, trustworthy partner in the public service experience. A leader's respectful presence assures community members that their interests are in capable hands, enhancing your credibility and strengthening professional relationships. This trust is vital in critical negotiations and high-stakes meetings where the confidence the public has in you can determine the success of your initiatives.

As a leader, you're the face of your agency. Your respectful professional identity reflects the agency's values and standards, reinforcing the agency's ethos. It demonstrates a commitment to excellence that permeates the agency, from the meeting room to the frontline of community service. By embodying the principles of respect, you elevate the agency's reputation, making it a preferred partner in public initiatives and a trusted entity among communities.

As a leader, when you broadcast respect for yourself and others through your look of leadership, you establish an uncompromising benchmark. But just like the journey of a boomerang, respect in leadership is influenced by the one holding it.

It's a Sign of Self-Respect

What's your job title? I already know. All of my readers have one thing in common—they're chief executive officers. Surprised? Or are you disappointed that you can't find this title on your business card yet? Let me explain: In my understanding, you're a CEO right now—the CEO of your professional identity, the CEO of your brand and reputation, the CEO of your career. You have the power to shape it as you wish—or let it slip away. No one is coming to rescue you. You're the most important element in your journey, so there's no one you need to respect more than yourself.

Self-respect is about acknowledging your inherent worth without displaying self-importance. It manifests in the meticulous care you take in your appearance, reflecting an inner ethos of precision and attention to detail. Picture a veteran government administrator whose impeccable business attire demands attention, from senior leaders to frontline employees. Or picture a director of public health initiatives whose refined attire personifies their investment in projecting confidence and authority during critical community briefings. Their self-respect radiates outward through thoughtful material selections, cohesive sophistication in styling, and a prioritization of impeccable tailoring and grooming. Even the most subtle accessories and accents broadcast their respected leadership and credible authority.

Self-respect is a visual representation of your professional ethos. At its core, cultivating a respectful professional identity means ensuring every detail is curated with zeal, precision, and philosophical conviction. Every component must integrate seamlessly within the greater story you seek to inspire, underscoring your unwavering self-respect as a guide worthy of being followed. This armor of self-respect isn't rooted in vanity. It's the outward personification of the diligence earned through years of excellence in the public service battlegrounds.

Self-respect requires relentless dedication but not extravagance. Dressing with self-respect isn't about flaunting expensive labels or wealth, but let's be practical: Investing in your wardrobe is an act of self-valuation. It's a commitment to the mindset that representing yourself, your team, and your agency's priorities at the highest level is worth the investment and is not an indulgent afterthought. It's about allocating resources wisely to secure components that empower you to look and feel like the respected force your agency deserves.

Self-respect extends beyond material investments to include time and effort. Relentless dedication to self-respect in your visual presence isn't just about looking good, it's about embodying leadership principles, discipline, and self-worth. It's a visual affirmation of your readiness to lead, inspire, and achieve at the highest levels in public service and operational excellence. This commitment to self-respect ensures you're willing to take the time and make the effort to always prepare to face challenges with poise and confidence, reinforcing your position as a leader in service and duty, one who commands respect and admiration.

Self-respect involves consistency. Consistency in your visual presence, whether in formal meetings or casual settings, showcases your reliability and steadfastness. It signals that you're dependable and unwavering in your professional standards. By presenting your visual presence consistently you create a stable and predictable professional identity that others can rely on. This steadfastness enhances your credibility and inspires confidence in those who work with and for you.

Self-respect includes taking care of your physical and mental health. A healthy leader reflects discipline and self-care, crucial aspects of self-respect that contribute to your professional identity. Physical well-being isn't just about aesthetics; it's also about the vitality and energy you bring into every interaction with team members, colleagues, senior leaders and constituents.

Maintaining a vibrant and energetic presence enhances your leadership by showcasing your ability to manage and prioritize your health amidst the demanding professional requirements of service and duty roles. Mental health is equally significant in leadership. A calm and composed demeanor reflects inner strength and stability, essential traits for any leader in the high-pressure public sector environment. Prioritizing mental clarity ensures you can navigate challenges and make decisions with a level head and a confident mind. By exuding physical health and mental clarity, you project an image of resilience and reliability that forms a critical part of your professional identity. It translates into a confident and commanding presence, making you a more effective and inspiring leader.

Embracing self-respect transforms not only how others see you but also how you see yourself. It fosters a sense of purpose and fulfillment that transcends external validations. True leadership begins within and, by cultivating self-respect, you unlock the potential to lead with authenticity, inspire with integrity, and achieve with resolve. Remember, no one will rescue you. You're the CEO of your professional identity, your brand, and your public sector career. The power to cultivate self-respect is in your hands. Ultimately, the greatest testament to your leadership will not be the accolades you receive but the respect you earn, starting with the respect you give yourself.

Self-respect Shows You Respect Others

Although self-respect is your foundation, no leader acts in a vacuum. Your influence extends far beyond yourself, shaping the perceptions and experiences of those around you. The way you present yourself is a powerful communication tool that conveys your respect for others. In an instant, it communicates your intentions, impacting how others perceive you and the environment you create.

When you dress with care and intention, you signal to the diverse individuals and communities you engage that you value their perspectives and honor their contributions. By embodying respect in your visual presence, you set a tone for a culture in which everyone feels valued and empowered.

Your look of leadership impacts how your family and friends are perceived. The way you present yourself extends beyond your professional sphere and impacts how those closest to you are perceived. When you maintain a respectful visual presence, you honor the trust and support of those who are part of your journey. This broader respect reinforces the perception others have for your network, elevating the collective reputation of all connected to you. Your appearance serves as a testament to the values you share with your inner circle, showcasing a commitment to excellence that uplifts everyone associated with you.

Your look of leadership is a signal of respect to your team members. Your commitment to maintaining a respectful visual presence signals to them that you value their contributions and are dedicated to leading by example. This respect fosters a culture of mutual trust and high standards, encouraging team members to mirror you. By showing you hold yourself to high standards, you set a powerful example that motivates your team to strive for excellence in a cohesive, high-performing environment.

Your look of leadership reflects the values of your agency or department. Every interaction you have, whether internal or external, reflects on the agency you represent. By presenting yourself respectfully, you demonstrate your commitment to the agency's mission and vision. This commitment to upholding the agency's standards enhances its reputation and strengthens its position in the public eye. Your respect for the agency is evident in how you communicate its values and uphold its brand visually, ensuring your professional identity aligns seamlessly with the institutional identity.

Your look of leadership reflects on those who lead you. As a leader, your respectful visual presence is not just a reflection of your personal standards but also of those individuals who lead and mentor you. Your look of leadership sends a powerful message about the values and expectations of senior leaders—the elected officials, agency directors, or military commanders you represent. By maintaining a respectful visual presence, you honor the responsibility bestowed upon you. You demonstrate your alignment with their vision and your dedication to contributing positively to the agency's reputation.

Your look of leadership is a testament to your respect for your field of public service. As a representative of your profession, your appearance should reflect the highest standards of your sector. This respect for your field demonstrates your commitment to its principles and your role in advancing its goals. By upholding these standards, you contribute to the overall credibility and prestige of your profession, setting a benchmark for others to follow.

Your look of leadership signals respect and reliability to your constituents. A respectful visual presence shows you value their time, fostering trust and building stronger relationships. This respect is not just about looking great but about demonstrating you understand the importance of their needs and priorities. This approach not only enhances stakeholder satisfaction but also shows you value their trust and are committed to delivering exceptional service to your community or constituents.

Your look of leadership should honor cultural diversity. As a leader in a field that often engages with diverse communities, showing respect for cultural differences in your visual presence demonstrates your commitment to inclusivity. By acknowledging and celebrating cultural diversity, you create an atmosphere in which all team members and community members can feel valued and respected. This respect is reflected in your willingness to learn about and adapt to various cultural norms and practices.

But this doesn't mean you have to dress differently based on every culture you encounter. Rather, you should ensure your look of leadership doesn't add friction points and respects the diverse backgrounds of those with whom you interact.

Your look of leadership should respect religious diversity. Recognizing and honoring others' diverse religious beliefs and values is crucial in today's public sector landscape. Your professional appearance should avoid elements that could be perceived as disrespectful to various religious practices and, instead, should reflect openness and respect. In doing so, you promote a culture of acceptance and mutual respect that helps ensure everyone feels valued, regardless of their religious or ethnic background. This sensitivity fosters an inclusive workplace where individuals feel free to express their beliefs and values without fear of discrimination.

Your look of leadership should respect generational diversity. The modern public sector workplace is a blend of multiple generations, and each one offers a distinct perspective. Respecting these generational differences in your interactions shows your appreciation for the diverse experiences and insights each generation offers. By presenting yourself in a way that bridges generational gaps, you foster an inclusive environment. This approach leverages the strengths and perspectives of each age group. Your look of leadership should demonstrate a respect for all generations, ensuring you're approachable and relatable to everyone, regardless of age.

Your professional identity should embrace gender diversity. As societal understanding of gender evolves, it's important to respect and acknowledge diverse gender identities in your professional appearance. This respect not only supports those who identify outside traditional gender norms but also sets a precedent for acceptance and equality in the workplace. It reinforces your commitment to creating a space where everyone can thrive, free from discrimination or bias.

By presenting yourself in a way that acknowledges and respects diverse gender identities, you foster an inclusive environment where everyone can feel valued and respected. In addition, you must ensure your look of leadership avoids reinforcing outdated gender norms and, instead, promotes a culture of inclusivity and respect.

The way you present yourself as a leader in service and duty is a profound act of respect that goes beyond superficial appearances. It's an affirmation of your commitment to the values and principles that underpin your professional and personal interactions. By consciously cultivating a look of leadership that honors the diverse identities and backgrounds of those with whom you engage, you create a powerful ripple effect that fosters inclusivity, trust, and collaboration. This dedication to respectful self-presentation not only enhances your credibility but also serves as a beacon of inspiration for others to follow. As you navigate the complexities of modern leadership, let your appearance be a testament to your unwavering respect for the humanity and dignity of every individual you encounter. This approach will not only elevate your own leadership journey but also contribute to building a more compassionate and connected professional world.

It's Not Always Reciprocated

Remember the boomerang we launched at the beginning of this chapter? Ideally, it gracefully returns to your hand but, as we know, that isn't always the case. Whose fault is it when the boomerang doesn't return? Is it the fault of the thrower, the craftsman who created the boomerang, the whims of the wind? The answer often is elusive. And the same is true for respect. Although we all hope respect will be reciprocated, that's not always the case. It might be your team member who shows up disheveled at a critical briefing, your own senior leaders who fail to represent your agency's mission with the necessary gravitas, or a colleague whose lack of professionalism undermines the efforts of a collaborative initiative.

As a leader who meticulously cultivates a respectful professional identity, it can be disheartening to encounter individuals who don't extend the same courtesy. And there also are the too frequent occasions when members of the public engage with you in ways that fall far short of the respect you deserve. These interactions, though unfortunate, are often rooted in the emotionally charged nature of your work and the public's frustrations or misconceptions about government and political influences. It's vital to remember that these moments are rarely personal but rather reflections of broader systemic issues or general sentiments toward agencies. Keeping this in mind can help you navigate these exchanges without internalizing the negativity.

In the following we'll focus on internal incidents—those that occur within your team and within your agency—when respect isn't reciprocated. Understanding why this happens and how to navigate these challenges without compromising your own standards is essential for sustaining your integrity and leadership. Just as we might have some ideas about why that boomerang didn't return, there are plenty of potential reasons others may not reciprocate the respect you consistently demonstrate. We'll examine some of those reasons now.

Lack of awareness: Some professionals may simply be unaware of the importance of maintaining a respectful appearance in professional settings. They might not recognize how their visual appearance affects others or understand the impact of a respectful look of leadership. This lack of awareness can lead to unintentional disrespect, stemming from ignorance rather than malice. It's essential to understand that these individuals might not be acting out of ill will but rather from a place of unfamiliarity with professional standards.

Different standards: Unfortunately, not everyone adheres to the same standards of visual appearance. Some may prioritize their own interests above mutual respect, displaying a lack of consideration in their appearance that is self-serving or inconsiderate.

Such actions undermine the collective effort and can create an atmosphere of resentment. As a leader, it's crucial to set and uphold high professional standards, reinforcing the importance of maintaining a respectful and professional appearance to better achieve shared institutional goals.

Personal context: You never know the full story. It's important to remember that everyone has a unique story and context that may not be immediately visible. Personal struggles, health issues, cultural differences, or challenging circumstances—all can influence how people present themselves. You must be careful not to jump to conclusions or make assumptions about someone's lack of respect based solely on their appearance. Instead, approach these situations with empathy and understanding, recognizing there may be unseen factors at play.

External pressures: External pressures, such as tight deadlines, emergencies, or high-stress situations common in public service roles can impact how professionals present themselves. These pressures might lead to moments when maintaining a respectful appearance is not a priority. Although you need to show understanding for these temporary lapses, it's important to ensure they are only temporary.

Personal insecurities: Professionals who are insecure about their own appearance may exhibit disrespectful actions as a defensive mechanism. They might feel threatened by your look of leadership, leading them to undermine or dismiss your efforts in an attempt to bolster their own self-esteem. Understanding that such behavior often stems from a place of insecurity allows you to address it with empathy rather than frustration.

Economic constraints: Not everyone has the same financial resources to invest in a professional wardrobe. Economic constraints can affect how professionals present themselves, leading to differences in appearance that might be mistaken for a lack of respect.

Although someone's financial limitations are difficult for you to change, it's important to create an understanding that a respectful visual appearance doesn't mean you have to break the bank.

Environmental influences: Professionals might adopt a more casual or disheveled appearance because they see it modeled by others. This situation can create a vicious cycle in which a lack of attention to visual appearance becomes normalized, eroding respect. As a leader, it's vital to recognize the impact of the agency or department's culture and work proactively to cultivate a more respectful environment. This effort includes setting clear expectations for appearance, modeling a respectful look of leadership and addressing issues of neglect promptly and effectively.

Rebellion against norms: Like it or not, some professionals might intentionally reject conventional standards of respectful appearance as a form of personal expression or rebellion against what they perceive as outdated norms. It can be a conscious choice to challenge the status quo and advocate for a more relaxed or inclusive definition of professionalism. There's not much you can do other than respect their choice and maintain your own standards. If they're in your sphere of influence, you can continue to mentor them. You also may have to reconsider whether they're the right person for their role.

Maintaining your own standards of respect, even when it's not reciprocated, is an act of resilience and integrity. It's a testament to your character and commitment to leadership excellence. This steadfast adherence to your values, even when it's not reciprocated, sets you apart as a true leader in service and duty.

Respect is not merely an exchange but a reflection of your inner ethos. It's a gift to yourself and those you lead, regardless of whether it's reciprocated. So never relinquish your own standards, no matter how much you're tested.

Damage Control: When Things Go Wrong

When someone throws a boomerang it can veer off course and cause a moment of panic. It might narrowly miss someone's face or, worse, actually strike them. It's a stark reminder that, even with the best intentions, things can go wrong. And just like with a boomerang, our actions can sometimes have unintended consequences. The spectrum of potential missteps is vast. It can range from minor slip-ups, like arriving a few minutes late to a critical briefing or forgetting to silence your phone during an important public meeting, to more significant blunders like making an insensitive comment to a diverse group of community members, or making a well-intended joke that falls flat.

In extreme cases, a severe lapse in judgment or a major ethical violation could escalate into a full-blown crisis, potentially risking your entire agency's reputation. Regardless of the scale, when our professional identity takes a hit, the damage can be profound. It's not just about a momentary embarrassment; it's about the long-term erosion of trust, credibility, and respect that you've worked so hard to build in a sector centered on public trust and service excellence.

In public interactions, mistakes carry an additional layer of risk in today's interconnected world. You constantly face the possibility that individuals will share their experiences with the world, and there's little you can do about it. This sharing can take many forms, each with its own potential for widespread impact. A community member might post about their experience on their private social media profiles, reaching friends and family who trust their opinion. They might leverage platforms to leave feedback, influencing countless others who rely on such sites for decision-making. With smartphones almost always at hand, individuals can capture moments instantly, turning a minor incident into a lasting digital record. Some might even go so far as to live-stream incidents, broadcasting your misstep to a potentially global audience.

In the public sector, this dynamic becomes even more pronounced. Leaders and professionals in roles like law enforcement, public administration, or emergency services often find themselves at the center of emotionally charged situations. The public's perception of these roles—often shaped by media narratives or experiences—can amplify scrutiny, making even minor incidents subject to intense debate and discussion.

Consider the viral nature of interactions involving law enforcement or government offices. A single moment captured on video, perhaps taken out of context, can rapidly escalate into a public relations crisis. The challenge lies in the emotional intensity of these exchanges. When constituents feel their concerns haven't been adequately addressed or perceive an injustice, they may turn to social media for recourse. This instinct to "share their side" often bypasses traditional channels for resolving grievances, creating a situation in which context, intent, and nuance are lost in the court of public opinion.

Such actions can create a ripple effect far beyond your control. Your agency could lose potential allies it never knew it had a chance to secure. The bandwagon effect in people's minds creates the illusion that "if my friend had this experience, it must be true, and I won't risk having the same." This mentality can lead to a cascade of lost opportunities. Moreover, in our viral-driven world, negative experiences usually spread quickly, potentially damaging your agency's reputation on a global scale within mere hours.

On the other hand, mistakes in interactions with team members, while often less public, can have equally serious consequences. These internal missteps can slowly erode the foundation of your agency. Team morale and trust may wane as team members feel undervalued or misunderstood. Moreover, team members often look to leaders for cues on acceptable behavior. If a leader fails to model respect and accountability, it can normalize unprofessional conduct within the team. This situation creates a downward spiral where the team's standards of collaboration and professionalism deteriorate, making it increasingly difficult to foster a high-performing and cohesive culture.

In both public and internal scenarios, when our professional identity takes a hit, the damage can be profound. It's not just about momentary embarrassment, it's about the long-term erosion of trust, credibility, and respect that you've worked so hard to build.

So you've made a mistake, and now you're facing the daunting task of damage control. How do you navigate these delicate situations and start rebuilding those vital bridges of trust and respect? First, avoid these two common pitfalls:

Ignoring the problem and hoping it will go away. You might feel like you're not responsible for how others feel and, therefore, choose to ignore the issue and move on. But by doing so you're losing control over the situation and its outcome. You can't be sure if the other party will move on, forget about it, forgive you, or share with others how you supposedly made them feel. Remember, your professional identity is not just what people tell you to your face; it's what they say about you behind your back. If you don't take control of your professional identity, others will shape it for you. The tension between your belief that an apology isn't necessary and others thinking you don't own your mistakes can create a toxic work environment.

A hollow apology is just as bad as none. The second mistake often made, particularly if you don't feel entirely responsible for what happened, is to blurt out a quick "sorry" when the other party might expect a more genuine apology. This can make them dislike or distrust you even more, as it suggests you haven't taken the issue seriously enough. If you believe an apology is in order, it's crucial to deliver it with sincerity and thoughtfulness.

When it comes to interacting with the public after a mistake has been made, the stakes are often higher and the situation more delicate. In the public sector, public trust is paramount, and a single misstep can potentially tarnish not only your personal reputation but also that of your agency.

And it's important to acknowledge that the strategies discussed here are most applicable to day-to-day missteps, minor incidents, and misunderstandings that arise naturally in the course of public service work. For example, addressing a constituent's frustration after a delayed response at a government office or clarifying an unintended miscommunication with a team member can be managed effectively with the principles outlined in this chapter.

When it comes to larger-scale incidents, particularly those that have escalated publicly or involve significant ethical, legal, or community trust issues, the approach must shift. In such cases it's essential to involve appropriate experts such as public relations specialists, legal advisors, or crisis management professionals within your agency. These experts can help ensure that your response is not only thorough and appropriate but also aligned with broader institutional protocols and the public's expectations. Think, for instance, of high-profile incidents involving law enforcement where videos of interactions have gone viral. In such situations, crafting a response without professional guidance can risk further damaging trust or inflaming tensions. Knowing when to seek expertise is as much a part of effective leadership as is addressing day-to-day challenges.

The first rule when dealing with the public is to act swiftly. Unlike with team members when you might have the luxury of a cooling-off period, public issues often require immediate attention. Time is of the essence, as a dissatisfied member of the public might escalate their grievance, contact media outlets, or worse, share their negative experience online before you've had a chance to make amends. Approaching a member of the public after a mistake requires a delicate balance of professionalism and genuine empathy. Your demeanor should convey that you take their dissatisfaction seriously but also that you're confident in your ability to rectify the situation. Remember, the public is not just looking for a solution; they're looking for reassurance that their concerns are being heard and addressed, and in the best case, that they can trust you and your agency moving forward.

In these situations, it's crucial to empower your team to act decisively. A frontline team member should feel confident in their ability to offer immediate remedies, whether it's providing additional assistance, clarifying a misunderstanding, or sending the issue to the appropriate department. The goal is to transform a negative experience into a positive memory of responsive and effective public service.

When you, as a leader, need to step in, it's important to personalize your approach. High-stakes situations or interactions with influential community members might warrant direct engagement from leadership. In these cases, a personal touch can go a long way. A handwritten letter, a face-to-face meeting, or even a follow-up call after the incident can demonstrate the high level of care your agency provides. It's also important to remember that the impact of a mistake can extend beyond the immediate individual involved. Others, including bystanders, might witness the incident or its aftermath. How you handle the situation can influence their perception of your agency as well. Lastly, view each interaction after a mistake as an opportunity for improvement. Gather detailed information about what went wrong and why. This data is invaluable for preventing similar issues and for training your team on how to handle comparable situations.

With these considerations in mind, let's take a closer look at how a proper apology should be executed, keeping in mind that while the following steps are framed in the context of internal missteps, many of these principles apply equally to public interactions, but with the added urgency and public relations focus that public service demands. Here are some effective strategies you can try:

Begin with self-forgiveness. This might sound trivial, but it's a crucial first step. Forgive yourself. Everyone makes mistakes, and everyone has off days. You've likely had to apologize for something at some point in your career. The key is to do your best every day. How you go about making things right and growing from your faults says more about you as a leader than your original mistake.

By focusing on restoration and growth, you can shift your energy toward repairing confidence, not only in yourself but also in the agency you represent.

Assess the impact. Once you've let go of the self-judgment that's holding you back, do your homework. Analyze the situation and try to understand how the other party may feel. Ask yourself tough questions about what exactly went wrong, assess the consequences, and figure out how it could have been handled better. This will help you grasp the details of the misstep and enable you to craft an apology that goes beyond a simple "sorry." In addition, consider the broader ripple effects on the morale within the team, the perception within the community, and the trust in the systems you oversee when analyzing the full impact of the mistake.

Choose the right timing. The timing of your apology is crucial and can vary depending on the severity of the mistake. For minor errors, such as arriving late to a team briefing, an apology is expected and accepted quickly. But for more significant blunders, like mishandling a sensitive public inquiry or miscommunicating a policy update, you might need to wait a few hours or even a day until emotions have settled and everyone involved is ready to process the situation and accept an apology. Sometimes, you might even want to coordinate the timing with relevant departments to align with institutional protocols.

Opt for one-on-one conversations. When planning your apology, keep in mind that this conversation should happen privately in a one-on-one setting. If your apology involves sensitive topics like inappropriate behavior, ethical concerns, or violations of policy, it's best to immediately seek guidance from your HR department or legal counsel. In most other cases, always aim for a private conversation with the person you need to apologize to. Later, you can involve your supervisor or others, if needed, and share that you've worked things out.

Avoid technology if you can; prioritize face-to-face. Whenever possible, apologize in person. A face-to-face conversation is always better than communicating via text message, email, chat, or even a phone call. When you apologize in person you allow the other individual to hear your voice and see your facial expressions and vice versa. If you send a quick "sorry" message, you can't gauge their reaction. You hit "send" and lose control over the process. If an in-person apology isn't possible, a video call is likely your next best option. Keep in mind that your nonverbal cues are important, whether in person or on a webcam, and that everything can be recorded. This approach is especially crucial in roles where public accountability is central; your presence and sincerity can go a long way in reinforcing trust.

"I am sorry." Say it out loud, and mean it. Your apology will only sound authentic if you truly are sorry. This is the first step to regaining trust and accepting forgiveness. Take responsibility for your actions and claim the blame. Say, "I realize I made a mistake," or "I understand you were hurt." Own the errors you made without shifting blame onto someone or something else in an attempt to reduce responsibility. When trust in leaders in service and duty is at stake, a genuine and transparent acknowledgment of fault can defuse tension and restore credibility more effectively than deflection or evasion.

Avoid getting defensive or making excuses. Although it might be tempting to over-explain your actions, trying to justify why you thought your behavior was acceptable can make others feel like you still don't understand the problem. Simply admit what went wrong and show that you're not operating from your ego. In situations where clarity and accountability are paramount, over-explaining not only can weaken your apology, it also can give the impression of insincerity. Instead, focus on demonstrating humility and ownership.

Share your lessons learned. After acknowledging your mistake, share what you've learned and how you plan to act differently. Offer to resolve the issue or fix the error, if possible. If you can't do so this time, because what's done is done, explain how you'll prevent similar situations from happening. Ensure you're able to follow through on your commitments. People are often forgiving once, but it will be harder for you to recover if you make the same, or a similar mistake, again.

Listen more than you speak. Once you've said your piece, stop talking and listen. Allow others to respond to your apology and express their disappointment, feelings, or perspectives on the situation. Resist the urge to become defensive or justify your behavior in response to their comments. By listening deeply you demonstrate your openness to understanding the full scope of their concerns, an invaluable trait in roles that involve serving the public or supporting diverse teams.

Express your gratitude. To close the conversation and move forward, offer a simple thank you. Don't overdo it; just express your appreciation for the opportunity to discuss the issue, then move on. Dwelling on the same problem and rehashing the same reasoning repeatedly can cause the negative experience to become more entrenched in both your minds. Acknowledging their understanding and willingness to discuss the issue also strengthens mutual respect, laying the foundation for a more constructive relationship going forward.

Be patient in rebuilding trust. Perhaps the most challenging step is patience. Regaining others' trust requires perseverance and, most important, time. It's unreasonable to expect others to immediately trust you again. Give them the time they need, or you risk undermining the entire process. Eventually, you must let go of the experience. This encounter doesn't define you and will often linger in your thoughts longer than it stays with others. Learn from your mistakes, but don't allow them to consume you.

Throughout the process transparency, humility, and a commitment to change are leadership keys. Leaders must be willing to have difficult conversations, listen to feedback, and put in the hard work of rebuilding trust.

It's not easy, and it's not comfortable. But handling mistakes with grace, accountability, and a focus on repair is a hallmark of strong leadership. It shows you're human, yes, but also that you're committed to growth, to integrity, and to the well-being of those you lead.

In the end, your professional identity is not defined by your mistakes but by how you respond to them. So the next time your boomerang goes astray, remember, it's not about the error but about the recovery. It's about picking up that boomerang, learning from the throw, and stepping up to try again, this time with more wisdom and more care to get it right.

Chapter 7
Leaders Look Controlled

The More You Control,
the Better the Outcome.

Chapter 7: Leaders Look Controlled

As a captain of a ship, you must navigate the vast, unpredictable ocean. Every decision you make, every course you chart is critical. The ocean is full of challenges—unseen currents, sudden storms, and hidden reefs. Yet your ability to maintain control determines the success of your voyage. You must be constantly aware of your surroundings, vigilant about the state of your vessel, and ready to steer your ship through whatever comes your way. Similarly, maintaining control over your professional identity is paramount. Each action must be taken with intention. Every detail declares the control you possess over your narrative. It's a powerful statement that says, "I steer the course of my identity," and it speaks volumes about your self-assurance and the respect you command, silently yet resoundingly. Although not every perception can be influenced, neglecting to consciously craft your professional identity allows others to fill in the blanks, often with incongruent strokes. By intentionally shaping your narrative, you ensure it remains firmly in your hands, a reflection of your ability to guide not only your path but also the trajectory of those who follow your lead. Taking control of your professional identity is not an act of vanity but an act of strategy. It's an affirmation that, even though you can't control every perception, you can lay a solid, indelible foundation that resonates with the identity you aim to project.

Why leave such a powerful aspect to chance? Why permit happenstance to dictate what can be shaped with purpose and precision in your public service career? In a sector where the public places immense trust in its leaders, the ability to convey competence, authority, and integrity through your professional identity is a cornerstone of building confidence in the agencies you represent.

Like a skilled public administrator or government leader who strategizes and executes each policy move with precision and foresight, as a leader in service and duty you must embrace every tool at your disposal. Your career is not only a tapestry of roles and achievements but also of the conscious effort to sculpt your professional identity with intention. This process is a cycle that involves the following steps:

- **Self-awareness:** where reflection becomes as routine as weekly status meetings with your department or team.

- **Self-care:** where discipline in personal presentation is akin to fiscal responsibility or managing public resources efficiently.

- **Self-promotion:** where advocating for your achievements is as crucial as effectively communicating your agency's accomplishments.

By cultivating your professional identity with intention and control, you do more than advance your career trajectory, you lay down a pathway for excellence while reinforcing public trust and demonstrating the values of the agency or community you serve.

Self-Awareness and Self-Reflection: Controlling Your Inner Compass

How often do you wonder if your professional identity aligns with the perception others have of you? It's a critical question that every leader should constantly ask themselves. Understanding how you're perceived by your team members, colleagues, senior leaders, and the communities you serve can make a significant difference in your leadership effectiveness. This reflection isn't just about seeing your strengths, it's also about acknowledging your weaknesses and biases. By continuously questioning and evaluating your actions and motives, you can ensure your professional identity represents who you are and what you stand for. This journey of self-awareness and self-reflection is about taking control of your inner compass and guiding your path with intention.

Controlling your self-awareness means continually looking inward, asking tough questions about your motives, your own biases, and the impact of your decisions. It involves taking a moment after each event—be it a community forum, a team meeting, or a major policy decision—to evaluate what went right and what didn't. But self-awareness goes beyond personal reflection. It's also about understanding how your professional identity influences your agency's culture, about recognizing the pivotal role you play in your team dynamics, and about how that role affects public perception and trust.

This self-awareness should shape your look of leadership, guiding you to cultivate a visual presence that aligns with your role and the expectations of those who look up to you. Your look of leadership isn't superficial—it's strategic. It's about how your visual presence can reinforce or undermine perceptions of your competence, approachability, and professionalism.

Constantly ask yourself these questions: "Does my wardrobe convey the authority and expertise expected of my role in government or public administration? Is my look accessible and reassuring to individuals from diverse backgrounds in our

constituency or community? How does my style affect my team's perceptions of my leadership in public service operations?"

As a leader, your visual presence should answer these questions and reflect your core principles. It's about choosing clothing that not only fits you but also fits the moment and the mission.

Self-Care and Self-Discipline: Controlling Your Well-Being

Ever struggled to find the balance between taking care of yourself and leading others? Trust me. You're not alone. It's a common challenge that many leaders in service and duty face. The demands of leadership in this sector often can overshadow the need for self-care, but neglecting your own well-being can have serious repercussions.

Think about the last time you felt exhausted or overwhelmed: How did it affect your ability to lead effectively in a crisis or during a critical public initiative?

Just like on an airplane where you're told to put your own oxygen mask on before helping others, self-care follows the same principle: If you neglect your own well-being, it will affect your ability to lead. To be seen as capable of nurturing and guiding others, you must visibly take care of yourself first.

This isn't about being indulgent but about performing the fundamental maintenance that enables effective leadership. It signals that you're well-prepared to manage the multifaceted demands of leadership. It shows you understand the importance of balance and are equipped to handle the various responsibilities and individuals who rely on your guidance and expertise.

Discipline is the commitment to regularly maintaining these self-care practices and making choices that align with your long-term goals, even when they require sacrifice or delayed gratification. This includes habits like getting enough sleep, eating nutritious food, staying physically active, and practicing mindfulness. These activities are not luxuries but necessities that enable you to perform at your peak in the demanding and high-pressure world of public service.

Discipline, especially in self-care, also means setting boundaries to protect your time and energy. It involves saying no to nonessential demands and recognizing when you need to step back and recharge.

For many leaders in service and duty, there's an imbalance where the rigor applied to caring for others—the public and their team—isn't always matched by the discipline needed for self-care. Acknowledging and addressing this imbalance is crucial, because disciplined self-care is the reservoir from which the strength to lead others is drawn. Applying the same level of discipline to your well-being as you do to your professional duties is essential for your professional identity.

Self-Improvement and Self-Promotion: Controlling Your Narrative

Have you ever felt hesitant to promote your achievements for fear of being seen as boastful? It's a delicate balance that causes many leaders to struggle. On the one hand, you want to highlight your successes and the value you bring to your agency or institution. On the other hand, you fear coming across as arrogant or self-serving. But if you don't advocate for your achievements, who will?

Effective self-promotion isn't about bragging; it's about controlling your narrative and ensuring your contributions are recognized and valued. It's about owning your story and using it to pave the way for future successes. Remember, as the CEO of your own career, you control these aspects to ensure your professional identity and visual presence remain strong and dynamic and that they are known, seen, and heard. Ultimately, self-promotion means articulating your achievements, not out of vanity but as advocacy for the value you bring to your public service role. This approach paves the way for your advancement and raises the profile of your team's efforts, aligning with and advancing collective objectives. Still, many grapple with the fine line between being perceived as confident and being labeled as self-important. Concerns about backlash or being seen as not team-oriented add to this complexity, compounded by imposter syndrome that causes

high achievers to fear being exposed as frauds. Cultural factors also play a role because, in some contexts, self-promotion is seen as boasting. This belief can limit leaders' willingness to engage in self-promotion. But despite these obstacles, self-promotion is critical for your professional identity.

Self-improvement, in contrast, often translates into a relentless pursuit of perfection. There's an ingrained belief that, to succeed, you must not only match but exceed standards set by predecessors or counterparts—every single time. This drive, although admirable, can morph into an endless quest where "good enough" rarely is, and the goalposts of achievement keep moving.

This pressure to continuously strive for flawlessness creates an exhausting cycle of self-imposed expectations. The journey to your professional identity should be reframed from a race toward unattainable perfection to a journey of growth that values progress over perfection. It's about recognizing the merit in each step of your development, celebrating small victories, and understanding that making mistakes is a natural part of learning.

Always remember your approach to these topics directly influences your professional identity. Your look of leadership isn't just about the clothes you wear, it also embodies the confidence with which you share your accomplishments and the grace with which you pursue development. It presents in the assured way you carry yourself, knowing you've earned your place, and in the mindful choices that reflect a commitment to continuous improvement. It's about the care you put into yourself and the awareness that you deserve it as a leader.

You—and only you—are in control of your professional identity. Your look of leadership is a visible extension of your journey. Let it be armor of empowerment. This look—your look—of leadership isn't static. It evolves as you do, shaped by the choices that position you as an expert and the controlled steps of development that keep you dynamic and forward-thinking. It's a look that respects where you've been and anticipates where you'll go, all while asserting the undeniable impact you make every single day.

Be Prepared for the Predictable and the Unpredictable

Are you a planner? Maybe even a micromanager? I admit I like to have control. I like knowing what's ahead. I like having a plan. There's a certain comfort in feeling prepared, in anticipating every move and scenario. It's the reassurance that comes from having a road map, a clear path forward. But let's be honest—how often does everything go exactly as planned? How often do we find ourselves navigating uncharted waters, dealing with unexpected challenges that no amount of planning could have foreseen?

In leadership, this tension between the known and the unknown is a constant. The ability to face both the predictable and the unpredictable becomes a defining trait of effective leadership. As you stand at the nexus of daily challenges and dynamic shifts, the ability to anticipate and adapt is essential. Hence, your look of leadership should be curated not just for aesthetic appeal but for its strategic function. Curating it with intention is an exercise in scenario planning, a rehearsal for the diverse roles you play to align the tangible elements of your look of leadership with the intangible dynamics of your day.

Embarking on this sartorial strategy requires contemplation, a series of reflective questions that may guide your choices and ensure your look of leadership is congruent with your professional objectives. Consider, for example, the following questions:

- What's the big picture for my role today?
- What's the occasion—a press briefing, community meeting, or legislative hearing?
- Who will I be interacting with—community leaders, policymakers, or constituents?
- What will they be wearing?
- What will my senior leaders be wearing?
- What will my colleagues be wearing?
- What will my team members be wearing?
- Where am I going to be meeting—in a government office, a community center, or a courthouse?

- Where might I be heading after the meetings?
- How will I get there—by walking through city hall or traveling between different public sector sites?
- Who else could I randomly meet today—members of the press, senior leaders, or constituents?
- Which message do I have to deliver today—about public policy updates or crisis response measures?
- What scenarios will I be facing today?
- Are there cultural considerations or social norms to account for with diverse communities or constituencies?
- How might my schedule or travel impact my ability to refresh my look?
- Might I be recorded on video or photographed?
- How does my look honor the narrative I wish to convey about my agency's mission and public values?
- How does my look serve as a model for others?
- How can my attire make a statement about the inclusivity and diversity I champion?

The answers to these and similar questions form the cornerstone of your professional presentation. They guide you to select a look of leadership that not only matches the situations you'll face but that allows you to shine in those you weren't prepared for. By strategically planning, you're taking command of an element of your professional identity that's too often left to happenstance. It's an intentional choice, assuming the armor of a leader poised to tackle the day's challenges, both known and unknown.

It's Not Only about Clothes

Looking the part is merely the opening act. Although a professional appearance can open doors and instill confidence, it's the substance behind the style that defines a leader. A leader's visual presence is crucial, but it must go hand in hand with their behavior, communication, digital footprint, and environment.

These elements work together to create a comprehensive professional identity that resonates with team members and the public and reinforces a leader's impact. So let's revisit the other factors that are crucial for your professional identity.

BEHAVIOR: Ethics and morals form the cornerstone of leadership in this sector, placing leaders under a heightened level of public scrutiny. Every decision and interaction is measured, not just internally, but by the community at large. The higher the ethical standards you uphold, the stronger the trust you build, not just within your agency but with the public who rely on you. Any perceived lapse in integrity can have far-reaching consequences, potentially eroding the credibility of your agency as a whole.

Your behavior carries as much weight as your appearance in shaping your team's perceptions of your leadership. The way you conduct yourself—your actions, reactions, and interactions—becomes a living testament to your professional identity. In the daily demands of leadership in service and duty where challenges and opportunities often coincide, your behavior serves as a guiding light for your team members. It should embody the virtues your look of leadership suggests.

Consider the following: You may dress impeccably, with every detail curated to convey authority in a government agency, but if your behavior doesn't align with this presentation, your appearance becomes an empty shell. Your composed conduct amidst adversity, clear directives, and swift decision-making reflect the respect and control suggested by your professional appearance. You must be the steady presence in times of tumult, the clarity in times of uncertainty, and the empathy in every strategic decision you make.

If you present yourself as a confident, decisive leader through your visual presence but exhibit indecisiveness, lack of composure, or poor judgment in your actions, the disconnect between your appearance and behavior can erode your team's trust and respect. But if your behavior consistently aligns with the values and qualities suggested by your professional appearance, it reinforces

your credibility as a leader in service and duty. This consistency influences not just how your team perceives you but also how willingly they follow your lead and embrace collaboration. The tone you set through your behavior impacts everything from team morale to performance standards. Let your behavior complement your look of leadership, not contradict it.

COMMUNICATION: The challenge of communication intensifies in emotional and high-stakes environments where words spoken with the best of intentions can quickly be taken out of context. This dynamic is further amplified by the prevalence of recording devices and social media, creating situations where a single misstep or poorly phrased statement can rapidly escalate, reaching audiences far removed from the original context. Leaders in this sector must be exceptionally mindful of their words, ensuring clarity, empathy, and alignment with their professional identity at all times.

Effective communication is a nuanced art. It's not merely what you say but how you say it. Your tone, choice of words, and clarity in expressing your thoughts can alleviate stress or, if mishandled, exacerbate it in high-pressure public service situations. Your visual appearance opens the door, but your communication invites your team and the public in, offering them a seat at the table.

Imagine you're presenting at a public forum for the first time to introduce new community outreach protocols. Your crisp look of leadership sets a professional tone, but it's your persuasive communication that will be remembered. You choose words that inspire rather than just inform. You explain rather than just direct. You listen—truly listen—not only to respond but also to understand and connect with your team and the public. In these critical moments your ability to communicate with compassion and clarity can make all the difference in how your professional identity is perceived. Your communication is the audible manifestation of your look of leadership. When in harmony with your appearance, how you communicate establishes you as a leader who's not only seen but heard and understood.

But if your communication is unclear, contradictory, or lacks empathy, it can negate the positive impression created by your visual presence. If you look the part of a confident, articulate leader but struggle to communicate effectively, the disparity can undermine your team's confidence in your abilities. In contrast, if your communication skills consistently match the message conveyed by your appearance, they amplify your impact as a leader. Your words and your look work in harmony, making your leadership more persuasive and influential.

DIGITAL FOOTPRINT: The Internet plays a pivotal role in shaping public perception, often amplifying negative experiences more than positive ones. As noted earlier, a single misunderstanding or isolated incident, even when resolved, can be recorded, posted, and shared widely, creating a viral narrative that's difficult to control. Leaders must approach their digital presence with the understanding that it's not just a tool for communication but also a safeguard for their reputation. Ensuring consistency and professionalism across all platforms is vital for maintaining public trust. Your digital presence is a reflection of your reputation, expertise, and judgment. This digital reflection of you can either strengthen your team's and the public's trust in your professional capabilities or raise doubts about your fitness as a leader in service and duty.

As you navigate the complexities of your digital presence, consider the emotional contexts in which your digital presence might be scrutinized. Your digital footprint is not limited to traditional working hours. At any time, 24/7/365, others make assumptions about your professional identity by the digital breadcrumbs you leave behind. Even while you're leading a meeting, team members or constituents might be looking you up online, possibly right there in the room or during a break. They might come across your digital interactions and shape their emotional responses accordingly before they even engage with you directly.

That's why your digital professional identity should not merely be a shadow of your in-person identity, it should be its affirmation. Ensure consistency between your digital presence and your

physical presence to fortify your professional narrative. This congruence reassures your team and the public that the leader they encounter online is the same one leading the charge in the agency or the field.

If your digital presence is inconsistent with the professional identity you present in person, it can create cognitive dissonance for your team members and constituents. For example, if you maintain a polished, professional appearance at public hearings or official meetings, but your digital presence is filled with unprofessional content, inflammatory remarks, or inconsistencies, it can lead others to question your judgment, integrity, and reliability. Hence, aligning your digital presence with your look of leadership is crucial. It demonstrates consistency, authenticity, and a commitment to professionalism across all channels. When your digital footprint mirrors your professional appearance, it strengthens your team's trust and respect for your leadership.

ENVIRONMENT: For leaders in service and duty roles, perceptions surrounding taxpayer funding often add a unique layer of scrutiny. Many members of the public may view resources, office spaces, or even vehicles as being directly tied to their contributions, leading to heightened expectations of accountability and restraint. Although this perception doesn't align with financial realities, acting in ways that mitigate potential misunderstandings can preserve public trust and confidence.

Leaders must remain mindful of how their associations align with the identity they are striving to project, ensuring that personal and professional worlds complement rather than conflict with one another.

The choices you make, from the car you drive to meet officials to the books on your office shelves, contribute to the tapestry of your professional identity. Each decision, even if seemingly unrelated to your professional responsibilities, can color your team's perceptions of you.

Consider, for instance, the vehicle you choose. It's not merely a means of transportation but a reflection of you. An older, poorly

maintained car might inadvertently convey a disregard for modern efficiency. Conversely, a luxury sports car might lead to assumptions of extravagance that could cause others to question your financial priorities.

The layout and condition of your office project your style. Having an organized, aesthetically pleasing, and functional workspace not only enhances your productivity but also sends a clear message about your professionalism and attention to detail, qualities revered in any leadership role.

Think also of the individuals you associate with—friends, family, colleagues—their appearance, behavior, communication, and digital presence can reflect on you, too, positively or negatively. You're judged by the company you keep, so it's prudent to surround yourself with individuals who support and amplify your professional identity.

If your environment is at odds with the professional identity you want to project, it can create a jarring disconnect for your team and the public. In contrast, when your surroundings, associations, and choices align with the qualities reflected in your visual presence, it creates a cohesive, trustworthy impression. It shows that your commitment to professionalism is not superficial but deeply ingrained in every facet of your life.

Every aspect of your professional identity contributes to the overarching narrative of who you are and how your team and the public perceive you. Inconsistencies between your look of leadership and your behavior, communication, digital presence, or environment can undermine your credibility and effectiveness. By ensuring alignment and consistency across all these elements, you strengthen your professional identity, build trust with your team, and amplify your impact as a leader in service and duty. The situations you navigate may differ, but the emotional undercurrents of judgment and perception are universal, influencing how you're seen and understood in your leadership role.

Chapter 8
Leadership in a Digital Landscape

The More You Share, the More They Discover. The Less You Share, the More Suspicion You Invite.

Chapter 8: Leadership in a Digital Landscape

Gone are the days when the measure of a leader was taken primarily through a firm handshake or a direct look in the eye. Today, it's the digital handshake, be it a LinkedIn profile, a professional bio on a government agency's website, a glance through a webcam, or an introductory email that often precedes any physical meeting. For leaders in service and duty, this digital first encounter carries unique weight as it frequently influences perceptions of transparency, accountability, and competence long before any face-to-face interactions occur. A hastily composed profile, a poorly chosen profile picture, or an unprofessional post can significantly impact your professional reputation. Today, search engines act as the new background check, and your online identity speaks volumes, setting the stage for all future interactions. It's your digital breadcrumb trail that leads others to your professional doorstep—or not. It forms the narrative of who you are, what you represent, and how you conduct your professional life. A well-managed digital presence can open doors and establish a narrative of expertise and trustworthiness. Neglect it, and you may find that the narrative is written without your consent, shaped by others' interpretations and the whims of algorithms. The stakes are high. Your digital presence has the power to bolster or undermine the hard-earned emblems of your professional identity. For public leaders, this is particularly critical as their digital presence often serves as a reflection of the integrity and values of the government or agency they represent.

As a result, it's imperative you not only adapt to this digital evolution but also embrace it with the same level of precision and dedication you would apply to any professional endeavor.

- **Internal impact:** Your digital footprint carries significant weight in shaping how you're perceived by your team, colleagues, or senior leaders. A robust digital presence that showcases your best self can inspire confidence and respect among them. It sets a benchmark for professional standards. Conversely, a neglected or inconsistent digital profile may lead to doubts about your leadership relevancy and adaptability. In public service, this could erode trust in your ability to guide your team or uphold your agency's mission.

- **External impact**: Externally, your digital footprint serves as a critical touchpoint for the public assessment of your credibility and expertise. A well-curated digital presence that aligns with your professional acumen can significantly sway decisions and enhance trust in your leadership. Whether it's a voter seeking reassurance about your priorities, a community partner evaluating potential collaboration, or a journalist fact-checking your career, the narrative presented online influences how effectively you're able to engage with the public. Your digital engagements and the narrative they build play a pivotal role in determining professional relationships.

Your digital footprint is a complex tapestry woven from two distinct threads: the intentional and the unintentional. The intentional footprint is the result of your deliberate online actions and choices, whereas the unintentional footprint is shaped by the subtle cues and signals your digital presence emits. Understanding and managing both aspects is crucial for crafting a cohesive and compelling online narrative.

Your intentional footprint: Every click, post, and interaction within your digital landscape is a brushstroke in the portrait of your professional identity. This intentional footprint is about crafting a narrative that resonates with your leadership style and professional goals. It includes the profiles you set up, the content you create, the networks you engage with, and the professional conduct you maintain online. These deliberate actions are your direct voice in the digital world, offering a narrative that speaks to your expertise, your professional journey, and your thought leadership. Pause and reflect on the intentional echoes your online actions create. In the digital world, every click, post, and email contribute to the intentional aspect of your digital footprint. This footprint is a carefully crafted mosaic, each piece a deliberate action that creates your digital presence. The photograph you choose for professional community sites, the insightful articles you publish on public sector innovation or civic engagement, the supportive comments you leave on government forums are the brushstrokes of your intentional digital presence.

Your unintentional footprint: Contrary to the controlled narrative of the intentional footprint, the unintentional footprint consists of the passive signals your digital presence emits. These might include how frequently you update your professional profiles or the timeliness of your responses to constituent inquiries or public comments on official posts. This digital body language can also subtly influence perceptions of your professional identity. Just like body language in personal interactions, these digital cues provide a backdrop against which your explicit actions are measured. They whisper tales of your dedication to staying current and responsive in a swiftly evolving digital era. For leaders in service and duty, unintentional signals might include out-of-date information on a government website or unresponsive social media accounts that can create the impression of disengagement or inefficiency. The state of your professional profiles also whispers secrets about your attention to detail and relevance in a rapidly evolving digital landscape.

A profile with outdated information about your role or with broken links to your agency can inadvertently suggest a disconnection. Your tech-savviness—or lack thereof—is apparent in the way you navigate digital tools and platforms crucial to public communication and transparency. Do you leverage the latest features of social media, or do you falter with the basics of digital communication? And let's not forget the omnipotent algorithms of search engines. Your visibility or absence on the first page of Google search results can significantly affect your perceived credibility and authority, delineating a picture of prominence or obscurity. The silent symphony of actions and inactions forms the backdrop against which your explicit digital engagements are set. It's the combination of the overt and the subtle that collectively composes the full score of a leader's digital presence.

KNOW: Assessing the Scope of Your e-Shadow

The first step in managing your digital footprint is to know and understand what's out there about you. This initial phase requires a comprehensive analysis of your digital presence and utilization of search engines and social media platforms to obtain an unfiltered view of how you appear to the outside world.

Engage in a methodical search of your name—including the most common typos—and your titles supplemented by your role or sector and the name of your agency, department, or the fields you're connected with. Be sure your search spans all search engines, including Google, Bing, and Yahoo, to ensure thoroughness. This step exposes the full scope of your digital presence, revealing everything from professional milestones to personal moments that have found their way onto the digital stage.

To gain an unfiltered perspective of how the digital world perceives you, use incognito or private browsing modes, features available in most web browsers. This approach removes the personalization of search results, offering a clear, unbiased view of your digital footprint as it would be seen by someone encountering you online for the first time.

This step ensures you're not merely seeing a reflection shaped by your own online behavior but rather the raw results that are presented to the wider world.

Then proceed with an audit of your social media platforms. Begin with a critical assessment of your profile, profile pictures, and header images across platforms. These visual elements serve as the digital front of your persona; they often make the first impression online before a word about you is even read. Ensure these images are not only professionally appropriate but also convey a sense of your commitment to your public service role, whether through imagery that resonates with your agency's mission or a simple, dignified portrait that speaks of competence and trust.

Next, examine your handles, bio descriptions, and the content you've shared. This includes posts, articles, comments, and even likes. Each piece of content should align with your professional values, highlighting your knowledge, dedication to your work, and engagement with the broader community of your sector. It's about more than just steering clear of potential pitfalls such as controversial statements; it's about actively contributing to discussions and sharing insights that affirm your position as a thought leader and a reliable professional.

Equally crucial is the scrutiny of your connections. Remember, the company you keep can impact perceptions of your professional judgment. This is just as true online. Ensure your network includes only trusted friends and colleagues, sector leaders, and agencies that hold respect within your field of public service. This approach not only bolsters your professional identity but also cultivates your feed with pertinent, current information, keeping you actively engaged with the latest developments in your field.

In addition to general search engines, leaders in service and duty must pay special attention to role-specific forums, feedback platforms, or public review sites where constituents might reference you directly. For instance, a constituent might post, "The municipal director, [Your Name], handled my case with exceptional care." While this is positive, it also means your name is now associated with the department in a very public way—forever.

Conversely, a disgruntled individual might post, “I spoke with the public service officer, [Your Name], and felt ignored and dismissed.” This negative mention not only reflects poorly on the department but also directly impacts your personal professional reputation. Both scenarios illustrate why regularly searching for your name on public platforms and addressing feedback promptly is crucial.

Continue with your virtual meetings setup. These digital gatherings are not just a matter of convenience but a critical component of operations and team coordination. As such, ensuring a professional appearance and environment during virtual meetings is just as crucial as it is for in-person interactions.

Consider the visual backdrop of your virtual meetings. A cluttered or distracting background can detract from the meeting’s focus and diminish your perceived professionalism. Poor lighting can make it difficult for others to see you clearly, making communication less effective and, potentially, impacting the connection you’re trying to establish. Audio quality is another critical aspect. Background noise can disrupt the flow of conversation and hinder clear communication. Use a high-quality microphone and consider wearing headphones to minimize external noise.

In the digital era, written communication forms the backbone of daily interactions. Beyond emails and text messages, professionals engage in a myriad of digital correspondence, including project management tools, stakeholder portals, professional forums, and even comments on relevant online articles or blogs. Each platform and message carries the weight of your professional identity and requires careful consideration.

Always keep in mind that, in the world of digital communication, the reach and permanence of your clicks and words extend far beyond the immediate recipient. Leaders entrusted with confidential information or representing their agency must be especially vigilant. The potential for communications to travel unexpectedly is ever-present. Emails can easily be forwarded, and a message crafted for a specific individual or group can quickly find its way into unintended inboxes. Social media posts, despite the

illusion of control through privacy settings or the ability to delete them, carry the risk of turning into screenshots that can be shared. Once something is shared publicly, even with a restricted audience, there's no guarantee that the content won't be captured and redistributed. Even virtual meetings have the risk of being recorded without explicit consent. Third-party tools can capture audio and visual feeds, making any shared information, casual remarks, or discussions vulnerable to unauthorized distribution.

REPAIR: Correcting Your Cyber Image

This stage involves taking steps to mitigate any negative aspects of your digital presence—the "obvious problems." Whether it's unflattering comments, outdated images, misleading information, or more serious issues like unfounded allegations or the unauthorized release of information, taking decisive action is essential for maintaining your professional integrity.

When negative content is within your control, such as on your personal or professional social media profiles, websites, or blogs, addressing these issues can be relatively straightforward. This could mean removing or editing the content in question or updating profile details to better reflect your professional standing.

The challenge becomes greater when the adverse content resides on platforms or websites outside of your direct control. In these instances the initial step is to contact the administrators or content creators, politely requesting the removal or correction of the content. And be clear about the content's negative impact on your professional identity.

This effort might involve addressing misinformation or misrepresentations on forums, public review platforms, or even social media posts where constituents have commented on your role or on your decisions. These interactions require a delicate balance between assertiveness and diplomacy, recognizing that your responses might themselves be scrutinized by the public.

If direct requests are unsuccessful, or if the content's removal is complex, it might be wise to engage reputation management professionals. These experts are skilled in strategies to de-emphasize negative content in search engine results, making it less visible or discoverable by those searching for you online.

During this phase you also should confront the not-so-obvious problems. These are instances where the search results about you are not outright negative, but they don't adequately showcase your achievements or expertise or the positive characteristics you wish to project. A search result that isn't damaging but fails to showcase your qualifications or contributions to your agency or field of public service can be equally limiting.

The strategy is twofold: enhancement and creation. Start by enhancing existing content by contacting administrators or content creators to suggest updates or additions that more accurately represent your professional achievements. For instance, a public official might reach out to clarify their contributions to a local initiative or request that their agency's website include detailed information about their leadership role in a recent community project. Such enhancements not only correct potential gaps in the narrative but also provide clarity and recognition of your work.

At the same time, focus on creating new content that reflects your professional identity. This can include publishing articles on reputable sector-specific platforms, participating in interviews or podcasts pertinent to your area of expertise, or engaging in community programs that garner positive attention. Using social media platforms to share insights, joining professional discussions, and highlighting your contributions also can enrich the quality of your digital footprint.

Shaping the narrative around your digital presence is essential. Not only does it ensure your digital presence accurately reflects your real-world skills and values, but it also establishes you as a thought leader in your field of public service. This proactive stance ensures that, when others search for you online, they encounter a comprehensive and affirmative portrayal of your professional identity.

OWN: Claiming Your Virtual Real Estate

To address a potential problem, owning your name online is not just a matter of branding, it's a strategic necessity. A potential challenge arises when individuals share your name, a not uncommon scenario. From celebrities dominating search engine results to name twins with a more active digital presence, these situations can dilute your digital identity, making it harder for others to find the "real you."

To tackle this challenge it's crucial to establish a distinctive digital presence that clearly identifies you. This effort could involve using your middle name or initials in your professional profiles, incorporating professional titles or credentials, or choosing a unique version of your name that's linked to your area of expertise. These tweaks help ensure searches for your name lead to you, not someone who happens to share your name. Additionally, this strategy acts as a safeguard against future issues. The ever-changing nature of the internet means new figures can suddenly become prominent, perhaps eclipsing your digital presence.

For example, if a new celebrity with your name emerges, they could take over your search results. Or worse, someone with a negative reputation could impact the perception of your shared name. This is especially critical in the public sector where visibility and trustworthiness are paramount. Constituents might confuse you with another individual who shares your name, potentially affecting their perception of your credibility or integrity. Establishing a clear and unique online identity reduces these risks, keeping your professional achievements and reputation front and center.

So you need to go beyond merely setting up profiles on popular platforms such as LinkedIn or Instagram. You need to take a comprehensive approach to claiming your name across all digital channels to ensure that you, and only you, control how your name is represented online.

The process begins with registering your name on as many social media platforms, directories, and online forums as possible. Although it might seem daunting to maintain active profiles on

each, the goal isn't necessarily to be active everywhere but to prevent others from assuming your identity or diluting your digital presence. For leaders in service and duty, this is particularly important, as impersonation or misrepresentation can undermine public confidence and erode trust in your role. By owning your name on these platforms you create a protective barrier around your digital identity, making it more difficult for others to impersonate you or misrepresent your brand.

Furthermore, secure your domain name (e.g., YourName.com). Even if a website is not in your immediate plans, owning your domain is a crucial part of digital control. It blocks others from capitalizing on your name and sets the stage for a centralized space for your professional portfolio and contributions.

In addition, delve into niche platforms and professional directories tailored to government, public service, or your specific area of expertise, such as law enforcement, public health, or environmental agencies. These channels enable you to claim your name in more specialized areas and improve your visibility amongst team members, colleagues, senior leaders and constituents, acting as further validation of your professional identity and solidifying your standing within your professional community.

By taking these steps you ensure that, when you're searched for online, you present a consistent and controlled narrative that showcases the breadth of your professional life, visible not only to agency leadership, team members, colleagues, or constituents but also to the broader public sector network.

CONTROL: Commanding Your Digital Boundaries

Taking control of your digital presence extends beyond owning your name across various platforms; it's also about meticulously managing the nuances of your digital presence.

First, examine the privacy settings on all your profiles. Each platform offers a range of options, allowing you to control who can see your posts, can tag you, can comment on or share your content, and even who can send you friend requests or follow you.

It's essential to tailor these settings to suit your personal preferences and professional needs, ensuring your content is visible to the right audience while protecting your privacy.

And consider the implications of your current connections as well, because they can reflect on your professional persona. And be mindful of who you accept or seek out, because these connections can be viewed as an endorsement of your professional standards.

In the public sector, where trust and perception are paramount, your connections on social media carry even greater significance. Constituents, senior leaders, team members, and colleagues may interpret your network as an extension of your values and credibility. Managing personal social media when connections can become team members or constituents requires a delicate balance. As a leader in service and duty, it's crucial to understand that declining friend requests from senior leaders, team members, colleagues, or constituents is not only acceptable but often the most professional course of action. This practice of being selective with connections is essential for maintaining clear boundaries between your personal and professional lives.

Preserving your authority and professional identity is paramount. When team members or community members see your personal posts, they may alter their perceptions of you as a leader. Moreover, declining these requests protects your privacy and that of your family and friends who might appear in your personal posts. It also prevents potential conflicts of interest or the appearance of favoritism, especially when it comes to team connections or interactions with constituents. By declining these requests you avoid awkward situations when you might feel pressured to censor your personal posts or when a casual comment could be misconstrued in a professional context. Remember, declining a friend request is not rude; it's a professional boundary that many successful leaders maintain. If you feel uncomfortable about declining requests outright, an alternative approach is to maintain two separate accounts: one for personal use and another for professional purposes.

In this scenario you would have a personal account for family and close friends, and a separate professional account for work-related connections. This strategy allows you to have distinct profiles for personal and professional use. Because balancing personability with professionalism is key in public service, share enough to be relatable—perhaps a photo of an inspiring community event or a beautiful landscape from your latest site visit—but maintain boundaries. Avoid oversharing personal information or opinions that might alienate team members or constituents.

Moreover, be proactive in managing the content associated with your profile. Regularly review tags and mentions, removing or disassociating yourself from any content that doesn't align with your professional identity or privacy preferences. This might include untagging yourself from photos or asking others to refrain from mentioning you in certain posts. And again, think about the visibility of your likes, comments, and shares. These actions can be as telling as the content you post directly. They contribute to the overall narrative of your professional identity online, so it's wise to conduct these interactions with the same consideration you'd give to your own posts.

Finally, keep abreast of updates to privacy policies and settings on each platform. Social media sites frequently update their privacy features, and staying informed allows you to adjust your settings proactively, ensuring control over your digital presence. By taking these steps you not only protect your professional reputation but also establish boundaries that respect your privacy.

MONITOR: Persistent Surveillance of Your Online Self

The final step in managing your digital footprint is to vigilantly monitor your digital presence. Regularly checking how you appear on the internet isn't an act of vanity. Instead, it's a critical component of professional reputation management. There's no harm and no shame in frequently searching for your name in search engines.

One effective strategy is to set up automated alerts. Most search engines offer this feature for free and will send you notifications whenever your name appears online. This proactive approach ensures you're always informed about your digital mentions, allowing you to address any new content quickly.

If you work in a public-facing sector where community reviews or media coverage are common across search engines, social media platforms, or sector-specific sites, make sure to consistently review those too. Publicly expressing gratitude for positive feedback not only reinforces the favorable aspects of your work but also motivates others to share their experiences. Addressing negative comments is equally critical. Prompt and constructive responses to less favorable feedback demonstrate your commitment to valuing community input and to improving service delivery. This approach transforms a challenging situation into a testament to your dedication to community satisfaction and public trust.

In the fast-paced digital world, narratives can quickly spiral out of control if not addressed promptly. Being aware of what's being said about you online allows you to take timely action, whether it's correcting inaccuracies, responding to feedback, or updating your digital content to better reflect your professional identity. And although it straddles a fine line, keeping an eye on the digital activities of your team members, particularly in high-profile roles, also can be prudent.

As a leader in service and duty, you also must keep a keen eye on your counterparts and trends within your field to stay ahead of the curve.

Start by identifying your key counterparts or agencies, both locally and nationally. Follow their social media accounts, subscribe to their newsletters, and regularly visit their websites. Pay attention to how they present themselves online, the types of content they share, and how they interact with their audience. This can provide valuable insights into successful strategies you might adapt for your own digital presence.

In addition, monitor the communication and outreach strategies of leaders who inspire trust and credibility, even if they're not directly aligned with your area. How are they leveraging social media? What kind of content seems to resonate with their communities? Are they experimenting with new platforms or technologies? This perspective can inspire innovation in your own digital strategy. Remember, the goal isn't to copy them but to understand the digital landscape of the public sector and identify opportunities for your leadership to stand out. Use these insights to refine your own digital presence, improve your engagement, and stay ahead in the dynamic environment of public service.

Beyond the Basics: Unique Digital Considerations

Unlike other professions, every click, post, and connection you make carries a heightened significance, magnified by the unique blend of legal frameworks, ethical expectations, and public scrutiny that come with serving the public. Your digital footprint is more than a personal narrative; it's a testament to your commitment to transparency, accountability, and professionalism. Managing this complex interplay requires more than awareness; it demands strategy, precision, and vigilance. Here are critical considerations to help you navigate the intricate landscape of your digital presence with integrity and confidence:

You might not be allowed to have a personal social media profile. Depending on your role, restrictions or outright prohibitions on personal social media accounts may apply. These rules exist to protect operational confidentiality, maintain public trust, and prevent conflicts of interest. The risk is not just about accidental oversharing, it's about safeguarding sensitive information, avoiding unintentional bias, and preserving the impartiality required for your position. A single personal post, even unrelated to your role, could be exploited to undermine your credibility or the security of your work. The outcome? You avoid unnecessary exposure and ensure your professional integrity remains intact.

Your emails could become public records. Every email, text, or internal message you write might be subject to public records laws that allow constituents to request access to government communications. The risk is that even casual or routine messages could be taken out of context or scrutinized under the public lens. This level of transparency means you must approach every written communication with the mindset that one day it could appear in the media or public forums. The reason for this level of scrutiny is to ensure accountability, but the outcome for you is that you must exercise constant professionalism, clarity, and precision in your communications, knowing there's little room for error.

Your digital words during a crisis are the voice of leadership. In moments of public emergencies, your digital communication becomes a beacon of trust and authority. But the risk lies in missteps. If your messages are inaccurate, speculative, or lack empathy, they can escalate the crisis instead of resolving it. The reason this point is so critical is that, during emergencies, public confidence in government agencies hinges on clarity, reassurance, and precision. The outcome of managing such situations effectively is that your voice can provide the stability and guidance the public craves, reinforcing trust in your leadership and the agency you represent.

Every click, like, and share carries weight. Even the smallest action—a like, a retweet, or a shared article can be interpreted as an endorsement of ideas, biases, or affiliations. The risk is that your interactions, no matter how innocent or unrelated to your role, could be construed as partiality or unprofessionalism. This is significant because leaders in service and duty are held to a higher standard of neutrality and objectivity than others are. The outcome of managing such challenges properly is that your online interactions will consistently reflect your commitment to impartiality, reinforcing your reputation as a fair and principled leader.

Cyber threats are a constant risk. As a leader in service and duty, your digital presence makes you a high-value target for cyberattacks, including phishing attempts, impersonation, and data breaches. The risk is not just personal, it's also institutional. A compromised account could lead to widespread misinformation, security vulnerabilities, or reputational damage to your entire agency because of the interconnected nature of digital infrastructure. One weak link can have cascading consequences. The outcome of taking robust cybersecurity measures—such as using two-factor authentication, secure passwords, and monitoring for suspicious activity—is safeguarding both your personal and professional digital identities.

Your digital trail is an archive. Public sector roles often require compliance with laws mandating the archiving of digital communications, from emails to social media posts. The risk is that a casual or poorly thought-out communication could resurface years later and be taken out of its original context. The reason for this level of transparency is to ensure historical accuracy, accountability, and public trust. The outcome of proactively managing your digital communications is a reputation for integrity, ensuring your contributions remain aligned with your professional values.

Your personal posts will always be seen through a professional lens. No matter how private your personal social media accounts may seem, the public will inevitably connect them to your professional role. The risk is that even innocuous posts could be misinterpreted or weaponized to question your judgment or biases. The reason for this heightened scrutiny is the expectation that leaders in service and duty embody the highest standards of behavior, both online and off. The outcome of managing this perception effectively is that your digital persona aligns seamlessly with your professional ethos, maintaining trust and respect.

Self-promotion may be off-limits. Unlike in other sectors where sharing professional achievements is common practice, leaders in service and duty may face restrictions on self-promotion. The risk is that even well-intentioned updates about your work could be viewed as leveraging public office for personal gain, leading to criticism or mistrust. The reason these restrictions exist is to ensure public trust in the impartiality and integrity of service and duty roles. The outcome of adhering to these boundaries is maintaining the public's faith in your leadership while finding other ways to highlight your achievements through institutional channels or external recognition.

Your digital presence crosses jurisdictions. Your online interactions are not confined to your immediate community. They can be viewed globally. The risk is that content intended for one audience could be misunderstood or offensive in another context. The reason this matters is that leaders in service and duty represent not just their agencies but also the values of their communities, making cross-jurisdictional sensitivity crucial. The outcome of managing this issue effectively is that your digital communications remain respectful, culturally aware, and legally compliant, strengthening your reputation across all spheres of influence.

Whether it's through email communication, virtual meetings, or interactions on various digital platforms, each digital touchpoint offers an opportunity for you to reinforce your professional identity. It's not enough to curate a strong social media presence or a professional website; every digital interaction must be approached with the same level of care and strategic thinking. This holistic approach to managing your digital professional identity not only safeguards your reputation but also amplifies the positive impact you can have within your field.

Your look of leadership knows no bounds; it resonates through every pixel and screen and extends beyond the confines of your office walls or community meetings, casting a digital silhouette as vast as your ambition in public service.

Chapter 9
Leaders Lead by Example

By Changing Nothing,
Nothing Changes.

Chapter 9: Leaders Lead by Example

Like a compass in the hands of a skilled navigator, a leader's professional identity becomes the unwavering needle that points the way forward, steering their team through the challenges and uncertainties that lie ahead. A compass is a small but mighty tool, a symbol of direction, consistency, and reliability. It doesn't waver in the face of adversity, it doesn't bend to the whims of circumstance, and it doesn't falter in its purpose. It simply points true north, providing a constant reference point for those who rely on it. In the same way, a leader's professional identity serves as a steadfast beacon for their team, guiding them toward their goals with unwavering resolve.

Your paramount duty in your leadership role is to not only be that compass but also to create more navigators who can fulfill this role. It's also about cultivating more leaders in service and duty by demonstrating that exceptional leadership is less about dictating actions and more about setting a compelling example. By embodying those standards you wish to see, you become a leader in service and duty others are inspired to follow.

This approach is what distinguishes true leaders from mere managers. Whereas managers focus on ensuring tasks are completed, issuing directives, and adhering to the letter of the law, leaders inspire action through their own choices. They don't just tell their team what to do; they show them how it's done.

Great leaders in service and duty intuitively understand that leading by example is the most potent form of guidance that creates an unspoken standard, an organic dress code, a blueprint for behavior, a benchmark for communication, a template for digital engagement, and a standard for the living and nonliving elements that you surround yourself with in your environment that is far more influential than any written policy.

Your team members and colleagues are always observing, learning and, in many cases, emulating you. Being a leader means accepting that you're always on stage, setting an example for every person with whom you interact, from operational teams to senior leaders. And although it might sound obvious, every moment of the day it's crucial to ensure the example you're setting is a positive one. By practicing what you preach and paying attention to the minutiae of your professional identity, you not only enhance your leadership but also inspire your team to strive for the same excellence.

The flip side, being a poor role model, is the easiest way to undermine your own authority as a leader in service and duty. Does that mean you have to follow all the rules (and burdens) your agency puts on you? Maybe. Does that mean you can't have your own style and can't stand out and show your personality? Absolutely not.

Influential leaders are confident, and they trust themselves enough to live their own interpretation of a professional identity. They've put so much thought into it and created such a defined professional identity that their presence is instantly felt when they walk into the community meeting or department office. They're mindful of how others could perceive them and of how they want to be perceived. If part of this professional identity-building requires leaders to wear business casual in a town hall meeting, they wear business casual. If wearing culturally inclusive accessories with their formal attire adds something unique to their defined professional identity, they embrace it. Influential leaders in service and duty exude confidence and trust in their ability to craft a distinct professional identity that resonates with who they are.

Courageous leaders in service and duty don't make excuses. Instead, they apologize when they've done something wrong, whether it's a misstep in community outreach or an operational oversight.

And usually people have the most respect for those leaders who don't hesitate to say "I'm sorry" or "I was wrong." But people have a hard time respecting those who look for excuses in advance. A leader makes commitments, not excuses. If team members see leaders display commitment and courage and take responsibility for their actions and choices, they feel safer and more assured in following them.

And the same is true for your team members. When it comes to their visual appearance, you too might be faced with a variety of excuses. Sometimes they claim it's too hot or too cold to dress appropriately for their role, letting the climate dictate their professional standards. Financial concerns also can play a role when some feel the pinch of investing in a high-quality wardrobe for work.

Time, that ever-elusive commodity, is another barrier. The hustle of daily life may seem to leave little time for meticulous planning of your appearance. Amid these justifications, a deeper thread of resistance emerges. A claimed lack of style sense becomes a shield against change, and the actions of other team members or colleagues—"They do it too"—serve as misguided validation. Geographic excuses, such as "We're in a small-town municipal office, not a capital city government building," highlight a misunderstanding that professionalism has a zip code. Venturing into the digital world, some diminish the importance of a professional digital presence with a wave of the hand, dismissing it as "just the internet." This underestimation overlooks the profound impact of digital impressions in today's interconnected world. These excuses, although varied, share a common theme: they believe professionalism is confined to a specific weather forecast, price tag, or location.

As a leader in service and duty you might find yourself entangled in a web of excuses as these justifications echo through the office halls and are whispered by team members at all levels of your agency. They observe their colleagues seeking loopholes in the standards that might justify their choices.

In this landscape of justifications and rationalizations, your role as a leader becomes crucial. Successful leaders in service and duty sidestep these excuses to send a clear message to their team members: professionalism is nonnegotiable. Rather, it is integral to the fabric of the agency and essential for individual and collective success in delivering exceptional service to the public. Sending a clear message to team members sometimes means having honest conversations with them about sensitive topics that can range from inappropriate clothing to personal hygiene, from mismanagement of emotions in interactions to unfortunate social media posts, from neglecting workspaces to disrespecting the public. Although these discussions may feel uncomfortable, they're integral to maintaining the professional integrity your role demands. And it's not uncommon for leaders in service and duty to feel apprehensive about raising such subjects. If you feel that way, is it because of the following issues?

- Your commitment to fostering a positive team environment, knowing harmony is pivotal to operational success
- An inclination to avoid emotional distress given your role that may be centered on support and development
- Concern over possible adverse reactions that could disrupt team cohesion
- The need to exercise authority while maintaining a non-confrontational stance to preserve team spirit
- A tendency to avoid uncomfortable situations, particularly in settings where team members work closely and collaboratively
- Finding the right words can be challenging
- Thinking you're entering a personal space by addressing these issues

But please remember that your fundamental goal is to support your team members' professional development, not to criticize them personally. Here's how you can approach these delicate conversations with confidence and clarity.

Begin by thoroughly preparing for the discussion: It's crucial to enter these conversations with a clear understanding of the issue. Start by identifying the problem with precision. Reflect on the consequences this problem creates, not just for the individual involved but for the entire team and the agency as a whole. If it doesn't affect anyone, there's no need for a conversation at all.

Determine who's directly responsible for the issue. It's essential to pinpoint when the issue first arose and assess its frequency. Reflect on previous attempts to address the problem and their outcomes. This preparation helps you approach the conversation with a solid background, making it easier to discuss potential solutions effectively.

Finally, assess whether this is a conversation you should have independently or if it would benefit from the presence of another party, such as a human resources representative or a senior colleague. This decision should be based on the nature of the issue, its sensitivity, and the potential impact on the individual or team.

Seek guidance before you approach: In any case, it's recommended you consult with human resources or a legal advisor, if you have access to such a source, because some issues carry legal implications and require a delicate approach. Before diving into conversations about sensitive topics such as alcohol, drugs, religion, ethics violations, violence, theft, fraud, harassment, or bullying, it's wise to consult with an expert. These experts can provide essential guidance on handling the situation correctly, inform you about any disciplinary actions that may be appropriate, and ensure you adhere to laws and policies.

Seeking such advice serves as a protective measure for both you and your agency. It helps prevent potential missteps that could lead to false accusations or lawsuits.

Addressing such matters without proper preparation and understanding of the legal context could cause significant harm.

Pick the best time and space: Selecting the appropriate setting for such a delicate conversation is critical, especially within the bustling environment of public service operations. These kinds of conversations should never occur in public spaces like municipal buildings or public waiting areas where there's a risk of being overheard or observed by constituents or other team members, compromising the privacy and dignity of the team member involved.

Instead, opt for a quiet, private space where confidentiality can be maintained—perhaps your office or a secluded meeting room. This environment ensures both you and the team member feel secure, won't be distracted, and can speak openly without fear of interruptions.

Additionally, choosing the right moment can significantly impact the receptiveness and outcome of the discussion. Avoid scheduling these talks during peak operational hours or just before or after stressful shifts, because stress levels and distractions can hinder the effectiveness of your message.

Instead, find a time when you and the team member are least likely to be under immediate pressure, allowing for a more calm and constructive exchange. Also, you don't want to rush through this conversation, because doing so could lead to misunderstandings or the feeling that the issue isn't being taken seriously.

Bring yourself into the right mindset: Remember that these conversations are not personal attacks against your team member. They're meant to be constructive and help your team member and agency improve. Also, remember that neither of you is probably looking forward to this conversation. It's likely your team member is just as anxious as you are. So take a few minutes to clear your head and remind yourself of that objective.

Start the conversation with positive reinforcement: Doing so instantly reaffirms the value of your team member, especially if you share praise about measurable achievements. This could include citing specific instances in which their attention to detail improved community satisfaction, their quick thinking averted a potential public service failure, or their insights led to a significant improvement in operational efficiency.

Conversely, vague compliments like "You're doing great" or "We appreciate your hard work" lack the specificity needed to make the individual feel genuinely recognized. Such statements, although well-intentioned, fail to highlight the unique contributions of the team member and can, in the end, turn against you: "Well, you said I'm doing great, so what's the point?"

Focusing on concrete achievements sets a constructive tone, demonstrating you value their contributions in a specific area while allowing there's room for improvement in another.

Use neutral and straightforward language: When addressing concerns it's crucial to be clear and precise to ensure there's no room for misunderstanding. For instance, instead of saying, "Your outfits are inappropriate," you need to be specific: "I've noticed that your wardrobe choices, particularly in terms of interaction with the public, may not align with our agency's expectations. This is especially true when you wear xyz." This approach makes your feedback not only more actionable but also less personal and more focused on professional standards.

Aim for a delivery that's straightforward and unembellished yet sensitive. Let the facts speak for themselves and calmly present them without the distortion of emotional undercurrents. This ensures feedback is received as intended—as a means to maintain professional standards and uphold the agency's reputation rather than as a personal critique.

Don't refer to others: When you need to address a team member's conduct, center the conversation on your own observations and experiences rather than on third-party comments or hearsay.

It's crucial to base your conversation on incidents you've witnessed, not on anecdotes or grievances passed on by others. If the situation occurred in your absence or cannot be personally verified, ensure you have written, verifiable evidence to substantiate your points. This approach not only preserves the dignity of your team members but also maintains the credibility of your leadership in the eyes of those you serve.

Describe the consequences for them and your agency: Articulate the impact on their own reputation and the broader impact of their actions. For instance, explain how their choices not only hamper their own professional growth but also tarnish the collective reputation of the team, department, and agency. This perspective shift helps team members understand the gravity of the situation beyond their individual sphere. For example, a recurring failure to meet deadlines might not only delay critical public services but also diminish trust among your team and constituents, affecting the agency's ability to fulfill its mission.

But address these concerns without making it about your personal grievances (i.e., "I" statements). The focus should remain on the consequences of their actions on themselves and the agency, not on you as an individual leader. This approach ensures the feedback is purposeful and targeted toward fostering an environment in which their own well-being and the highest levels of public service excellence are maintained.

Be clear about how you would like them to change: Rather than dwell on the past, move quickly to the future, but don't expect your team member to know exactly what you expect them to change. For instance, if a team member has repeatedly shown unprofessional behavior when addressing the public, don't just highlight those lapses.

Instead, clearly outline the steps for improvement, such as adhering to a specific protocol for public interactions, providing exact timelines for completing assigned tasks, and committing to regular progress updates. Specify that these measures are nonnegotiable for maintaining the high standards of service and professionalism to which your agency is committed. Unless you're specific in your request, there will be confusion about what needs to be done (or not) moving forward.

Be careful when offering support: Although it's essential to be supportive, emphasize that the responsibility for improvement rests with the team member. You should be there to assist, but the obligation is on them. This stance prevents dependency and promotes accountability.

Be prepared for pushback: In fact, anticipate it, it's a natural response. But it's crucial to maintain your composure and keep the dialogue centered on the matter at hand. Instead of allowing their response to sidetrack the conversation, seize it as a chance to emphasize your expectations and the importance of meeting them. Pushback may come in the form of frustration, defensiveness, or even claims of unfair treatment, particularly in the public sector where accountability measures can feel heightened. Instead of leaping to defend your stance with rigidity, pause and truly hear your team member.

Misunderstandings, fear, or frustration often underpin their responses. Your attentiveness not only demonstrates respect for their viewpoint, but it also can diffuse tensions, paving the way for a dialogue that's both more constructive and collaborative.

Although you can acknowledge their emotions as a way to navigate through their initial reactions, seize the moment to once again clarify the issue, the solution you discussed, and the impact it otherwise has. By reiterating the conversation's objective—to foster their development and enhance overall outcomes—you underscore the collective aim of this exchange.

Remember, your conversation is not a personal critique from you and, similarly, their reaction is not a personal attack on you.

Summarize what was discussed and announce a follow-up: As you draw the conversation to a close, it's essential to encapsulate the key points discussed. This summarization isn't just about reiterating the issues but also about confirming the mutual understanding and commitment to the agreed-upon actions.

It's a moment to ensure no detail is lost and that both parties are aligned in their expectations and responsibilities.

Announcing a follow-up or a check-in at a specific date is the next critical step, one that underscores your dedication to the process, the individual's progress, and the overall success of your agency. But this promise carries weight only if it's fulfilled. Failing to follow through not only diminishes the effectiveness of the initial conversation but also erodes your authority and credibility as a leader.

End the conversation on a neutral note: The way in which such a conversation concludes can significantly influence the subsequent actions and attitudes of your team member. It's essential to strike the right balance in the closing moments, ensuring the team member doesn't leave feeling overly discouraged or burdened by the discussion.

Conversely, ending on an excessively optimistic note might dilute the importance of the feedback you've given, a phenomenon I refer to as "sandwich" feedback. When the critical message is sandwiched between two positives, it potentially lessens its impact. Aim for a neutral closure such as, "Let's go back to work," which signals the discussion is complete and is just one of many interactions you have in your leadership role.

Document the exchange: This ensures there's a clear record, safeguarding both you and your agency against future misunderstandings or disputes regarding performance or conduct.

Start by documenting who was present during the meeting, and capture the full context of the discussion. It's vital to include the date, time, and location to anchor the conversation in a specific moment and place. This level of detail provides a foundation of transparency and accountability for all parties involved. Meticulously record the meeting: What issues were discussed? What were the observations that prompted the conversation, the feedback you provided, and the team member's response.

Crucially, detail the agreed-upon actions, including who's responsible for what and the timelines for these actions. This clarity prevents any ambiguity about expectations and responsibilities, ensuring everyone is aligned on the path forward.

Furthermore, outline the expected outcomes of these actions. What changes or improvements should result from this intervention? This sets a clear benchmark for assessing progress and effectiveness. Finally, specify the follow-up steps, including who will carry them out and when.

Documenting these aspects creates a comprehensive and indisputable record of the conversation. This thoroughness underscores the gravity with which you, as a leader in service and duty, approach your role, demonstrating a commitment to fairness, transparency, and the growth of your team.

You may also encounter situations that fall outside your direct span of authority. Perhaps you're leading a project with team members who don't directly report to you, or you're in a matrix agency in which your influence is more lateral than vertical.

In the public sector these scenarios are particularly common as cross-departmental initiatives or interagency collaborations often require leaders to guide individuals who may not formally report to them.

In this case it's not recommended that you have this kind of conversation. Instead, engage with the individual's direct leaders, sharing your observations and concerns. A best practice is to bring documentation that underscores your concern.

Position your feedback not as criticism but as an opportunity for collective improvement, emphasizing the shared mission of serving the public effectively and upholding the agency's standards. In these delicate scenarios your role as a leader is to facilitate positive change indirectly, using your influence to advocate for standards that align with the agency's values and objectives. It's a dance of diplomacy that requires patience, empathy, and a strategic understanding of institutional dynamics.

As you can see, leadership is a journey filled with challenges and responsibilities. It demands courage to engage in difficult conversations, wisdom to navigate the limitations of your authority, and the vision to see beyond immediate issues toward the greater goal of positive change.

In this journey your professional identity is the compass that guides you and your team. It's the unwavering needle that points toward your true north. When the terrain gets tough and the way forward seems uncertain, it's your professional identity that keeps you on course.

So as you continue on your leadership journey, keep checking your compass. Make sure your professional identity is always pointing true north. When you inevitably encounter obstacles and detours, use your compass to reorient yourself and your team. With your professional identity as your guide, you and your team can navigate even the most challenging of public service landscapes and emerge stronger and more successful than ever.

Chapter 10
Moving Forward

Chapter 10: Moving Forward

In concluding our journey through leadership and the crafting of your professional identity, it's essential to recognize that enhancing your professional identity is not merely for personal gratification. Instead, it's a fundamental aspect of your professional development. This endeavor brings rewards that extend well beyond the surface. It influences trust within your network of public service professionals, team cohesion within your agency, and opportunities for career progression in the sector. The critical question now shifts from whether you should refine your professional identity to how deeply you can commit to ongoing improvement and the pursuit of excellence. In the dynamic landscape of the public sector where challenges and prospects exist side by side, the need to distinguish yourself—for the right reasons—is paramount. The capacity to set yourself apart through an outstanding professional identity is what differentiates true leaders, those who establish an identity that aligns with the values and goals of their agency, meet the expectations of their community, and support the ambitions of their teams. And, of course, such leaders value themselves as the great leaders they are.

In this book I have aimed to guide you through the nuanced dance of this professional identity, blending the science of first impressions with the art of a sustained imprint. From the subtle cues conveyed by your look of leadership to the profound influence of digital footprints, we have dissected many aspects, offering you a blueprint for intentional self-presentation.

Now about that potato chip on the cover: Did you notice it?

At first glance it may seem like a whimsical choice for a book dedicated to such a serious topic as leadership. Yet that potato chip serves as a powerful metaphor for the concept of identity, both personal and professional.

Imagine that we're embarking on a journey together through a bustling supermarket. As we navigate the aisles, our attention is drawn to the myriads of products vying for our attention.

The significance of packaging design becomes strikingly apparent—the strategic placement of brands, the few critical seconds that influence our decision to add an item to our shopping cart. It's in these moments that the familiarity of a trusted brand effortlessly convinces us to make a purchase, though the allure of a new product can attract our notice through meticulously crafted packaging.

Although they're often perceived as separate entities, the most impactful packaging designs demonstrate that thoughtful packaging can not only complement but also enhance the product within. The packaging's shape, size, colors, and imagery are all chosen to convince you to buy it.

Now let's pause in front of the snack aisle and stare at the hundreds of potato chip packages. Chip packaging offers fascinating insights into successful branding. Do you realize that every potato chip package has an image of a chip on the front? And notice how the most successful chip brands manage to communicate the clear promise, "What you see is what you get." The imagery shows perfectly shaped potato chips, which conveys the product's appeal more than any description could. It's straightforward, no frills, and shows the product in its most enticing form.

Yet there's a twist to this tale, as you know. The crumbled reality inside the bag doesn't match the perfection depicted on the outside. Despite not having a transparent section to preview the contents, we're drawn in by the promise of ideal, unbroken chips. And not just once—again and again we continue to buy them, even after we've become aware of the illusion.

The lesson is profound: a compelling external presentation can lead people to embrace you, even if the internal reality doesn't quite match (yet). Achieving the opposite effect is significantly more challenging.

For leaders in service and duty, the metaphor of potato chip packaging is a poignant one, reminding them of the importance of having a consistent professional identity. You must ensure your external presentation—your appearance, behavior, communication, digital presence, and work environment—reflects you in the best light.

Just as the chip bag's imagery promises a certain experience, leaders in service and duty must convey an identity that their teams and communities can instantly respect and trust. Although no leader is without flaws—comparable to the mix of whole and broken chips within a bag—it's the strategic depiction of your competencies and commitment to public service excellence that should be emphasized. Just as consumers come to accept the imperfect contents inside a bag of chips because they trust the brand, so too will others accept a leader's human flaws if they're convinced of the leader's dedication to their role and the success of the agency or community they serve.

Now let's take another look at the potato chip aisle and contemplate expectations. If I were to ask you to pick a spicy flavor of chips, most likely you'd subconsciously look for a red bag. Or if you preferred an organic variant, you'd probably go for green or brown.

Our brains are wired to associate specific colors and designs with certain product attributes. This principle of expectation extends beyond the supermarket aisle to the realm of leadership.

Just as we have predefined notions about product packaging, we harbor expectations about a leader in service and duty's professional identity.

Despite the diversity in leadership styles and personalities, certain universal expectations remain consistent. Just as the bold red packaging of spicy chips stands out to a shopper looking for flavor, leaders in service and duty who align their presentation with professional norms are easily recognized and trusted.

But there's space for individuality and a break from convention, like a neon-pink chip bag among the typical reds and greens. A leader in service and duty also might choose to deviate from traditional visual cues through distinctive clothing or an unconventional approach. This differentiation can attract attention, signaling innovation and drawing in those intrigued by novelty. But it also may miss the mark of subconscious expectations, posing a challenge to receiving immediate recognition as a leader in their professional field. Much like a shopper instinctively reaching for the familiar red bag, oblivious to a pink option, people often gravitate toward the comfort of what they know—traditional emblems of authority and expertise.

Finally, like well-established potato chip brands that are strategically positioned at eye level on shelves to be easily seen and chosen, influential leaders in service and duty naturally command a presence and often enjoy higher recognition, similar to products occupying premium shelf space. Conversely, less prominent brands—or leaders—might need to exert more effort to be noticed.

In public service environments, being at eye level signifies remaining at the forefront of your team members, colleagues, senior leaders and constituents, always ready to be selected for your visible dedication to excellence, professionalism, and service. This prominence isn't merely physical; it extends to the entire professional identity you construct as a leader in service and duty.

As this chapter closes, let the lasting lesson be the craft of your professional identity, the external manifestation of your inner capabilities. Let the professional identity you create stand as your unwavering representative, conveying expertise in public service, fostering trust, and managing the intricacies of leadership with poise.

Your packaging is not merely an aesthetic choice; it's a strategic tool that, when aligned with your skills and vision, can weather the storms of challenge and change. Let it amplify your strengths in public service excellence, not overshadow them.

As you move forward, may your professional identity resonate with intention, your leadership echo with impact, and your presence be felt, even in silence. Stand out not just to be seen but to make a difference, to inspire trust, and to drive progress.

Here's to the leader in you, packaged to perfection, poised for greatness, and perpetually ready to turn challenges into opportunities in the noble service of your community and country. Go forth and lead, not just with authority but with the magnetism of a well-crafted identity, one that's as compelling and multifaceted as the leader within you.

Acknowledgments

To the extraordinary individuals serving in the public sector:

Thank you for allowing dreamers like me to live in a country of endless opportunities. As someone who has realized a lifelong dream of calling the United States my home, I owe a profound debt of gratitude to each of you who dedicate yourselves to the principles of freedom, safety, and opportunity.

Thank you for keeping us safe. When others run away from danger, you are the first to run toward it, embodying bravery and selflessness.

Thank you for keeping us secure. You work tirelessly, often behind the scenes, to shield us from visible and invisible threats. Security is not something we should take for granted, and it is something you uphold with your unwavering commitment to us.

Thank you for protecting our freedoms. Through your service you ensure that the liberties we hold dear are preserved for generations to come.

Thank you for serving the public good. You are the steady hands and compassionate hearts behind the services that make our communities stronger, healthier, and more connected.

Thank you for upholding justice. You are the defenders of fairness, ensuring that every individual is treated with dignity and respect under the law.

Thank you for representing us with honor. Your actions reflect the best of who we are, elevating the reputation of our communities and setting a standard for others to follow.

Thank you for responding in our darkest hours. When crisis strikes and uncertainty looms, you are the first to step forward, offering calm, strength, and solutions. Your leadership reminds us that hope is never lost.

Thank you for sacrificing quietly. So much of what you do is unseen and unacknowledged. The long hours, the moments missed with loved ones, and the personal risks you take are profound acts of selflessness. Though these sacrifices are often invisible, their impact is immeasurable, and for that you have my deepest gratitude.

To every individual in every corner of the public sector, your work is often unheralded, yet its impact is felt everywhere. Your service is not merely a job, it is a calling. It is a choice to dedicate yourself to something greater, to build safer, stronger, and more unified communities.

As you close this book, please remember that your leadership ripples far beyond your daily tasks. It inspires trust, reinforces unity, and shapes the fabric of this nation. Never underestimate the power of your service. Your dedication upholds the ideals that make this country extraordinary.

I hope there are countless moments when the public recognizes and appreciates the profound impact you have on this world. But if there are times when you feel unseen or underappreciated, I want you to know this: I see you.

I see your dedication, your sacrifices, and your unwavering commitment to the greater good. I see the long hours, the difficult decisions, and the quiet moments of resolve that define your work. I see the way you carry the weight of responsibility with courage and grace, even when the acknowledgment you deserve doesn't always come.

You matter. Your work matters. And though the world may not always stop to thank you, I hope this book—and these words—serve as a reminder that your contributions are valued beyond measure.

With deepest respect and admiration,

Sylvie di Giusto

About the Author

International keynote speaker Sylvie di Giusto brings her expertise from a successful corporate career in Europe to every presentation. Formerly the head of a management academy and innovation hub, she has developed innovative leadership programs for high-end education through unprecedented training methods. As the chief of staff for the chief human resources officer of Europe's largest tourism and retail group, Sylvie coordinated all group-wide human resources teams and activities. Prior to that, at a consultancy firm she implemented online and in-person training and development initiatives for Fortune 100 companies.

Now extraordinary professionals at respected organizations around the world—including American Express, American Airlines, Hilton, Nespresso, Microsoft, Prudential, and even the US Air Force—trust Sylvie to help them make the right decisions to grow their brands and bottom lines. Building on her five cornerstones of modern emotional intelligence—visual, behavioral, verbal, digital, and social—Sylvie gives her audiences the Power of Choice, a conscious decision-making framework that allows us to understand our perceptions, choose our behaviors, and determine our best outcomes.

Sylvie is the author of *the Image of Leadership, Discover Your Fair Advantage,* and the upcoming *Make Me Feel Important*. Sylvie takes audiences on an entertaining, spectacular, and thought-provoking journey through the brain and mind, from the unconscious to the conscious and, ultimately, to the heights of personal, professional, and organizational success.

For speaking engagements, please contact Sylvie's wonderful team at sylviebooings@cmispeakers.com or call +1-403-398-8488.

Perception Audit

Take the free Perception Audit and unveil the image you project to the world in just fifteen minutes. Receive a personalized report that illuminates how others perceive your professional identity and learn to align your self-view with the impression you intend to make.

Are you ready to meet the *you* that everyone else sees? Please use the QR code below or visit sylviedigiusto.com/audit.

After you've gained the clarity you need to polish your professional identity and project the best version of you in the workplace and beyond, let's stay connected. Follow me on social media to join the conversation about *The Image of Leadership*.

- instagram.com/sylviedigiusto
- linkedin.com/in/sylviedigiusto
- facebook.com/sylviedigiusto
- youtube.com/c/sylviedigiusto
- tiktok.com/@sylviedigiusto

Your Voice and Our Collective Reach

Books—just like you—face perception challenges.

In a world where perception is reality, the value and impact of books are often judged by the quantity and quality of their Amazon reviews. So if this book has offered new perspectives or valuable insights, please consider sharing your experience online.

Your review not only helps shape the book's impact but also guides others to find the same resource you did. Your role in this narrative could just be the beginning.

For those who have found resonance within these pages and wish to spread the wisdom within their team or organization, I offer preferred customer pricing for bulk orders. Please reach out to my wonderful team at sylviebookings@cmispeakers.com or call +1-403-398-8488. Let's empower more leaders together.

Made in the USA
Columbia, SC
28 February 2025